TAKE THIS JOB

AND Love It

TAKE THIS JOB *AND* *Love It*

HOW TO
FIND FULFILLMENT IN
ANY JOB YOU DO

Matthew Gilbert

Daybreak® Books
An Imprint of Rodale Books
New York, New York

*For everyone out there who is doing the work
that needs to be done—in the Creator's eyes,
your value is truly inestimable.*

Daybreak is a registered trademark of Rodale Press, Inc.

Printed in the United States of America on acid-free ∞,
recycled paper ♻

Cover Designer: Andrew Newman
Interior Designer: Faith Hague

Library of Congress Cataloging-in-Publication Data

Gilbert, Matthew.
    Take this job and love it : how to find fulfillment in any job
  you do / Matthew Gilbert.
         p.   cm.
    Includes bibliographical references.
    ISBN 0–87596–477–X paperback
    1. Job satisfaction.   I. Title.
  HF5549.5.J63G54   1998
  650.1—dc21   98–4463

Distributed in the book trade by St. Martin's Press

2 4 6 8 10 9 7 5 3 1 paperback

Contents

Acknowledgments

Special thanks go to my editor, Karen Kelly, who planted the seed and allowed me to grow it to fruition; Antoinette Botsford, who shared with me some of her stories and helped me to understand the power and place of the storytelling tradition in both ancient and modern times; Margaret Rhode, whose own story of workplace spirituality in action provided important direction in the shaping of this book; and my wife, Nancy, whose support and many insights were blessings on the path.

Preface

In the late 1980s, I participated in a yearlong intensive program in which the primary goal was to find one's "life work." I knew that others had "graduated" from this program and were trying to do work unique to who they were. They created their jobs from inside themselves based on a vision or a dream, often secretly held. I really admired these people, knowing that I had hit a wall in my own occupational search, tired of bouncing from job to job and passion to passion, frustrated that I wasn't getting what I needed in terms of some indefinable satisfaction that I felt was lacking. I'd been, among other things, a dice dealer in Reno, a freelance writer, a massage therapist, a white-collar soldier, all of which ultimately failed me. The fault, I was sure, was in these jobs, and not within me. So the search went on.

I was confident that this new program would change things. It demanded more of me than I had ever been asked. There were challenges at all levels of my being: physical, emotional, psychological, and spiritual. I got involved in new projects, became active in environmental politics, had others of like spirit supporting me in my quest. I did everything I could think of to birth my true calling. When I finally completed my training, despite feeling good—even blessed—about what I had done and learned, I had to admit that no one thing had seized me by the lapels and said, "Matthew, this is it! Your real mission has begun!" Had the course failed me as well? Or—and this was a big "or" for me—had *I* failed? Was it me all along? Was I doomed to a life of aimless pursuit, a lifelong prisoner of the philosophy that stated, "If you don't know where you're going, any road will get you there"?

Now, 10 years later, I look back on that time and all that has passed since then, and I realize that in an unexpected way, I *had* discovered my true calling, which was less a calling than a discovery: Any road *can* take me where I want to go, as long as my destination is a spiritual one. And while our choice of jobs can make such a journey a little easier or a lot harder, almost any kind of work can be a place to learn and practice spiritual lessons. The challenge is to view it with new eyes, for whatever it is that one does, there is potential for doing it better, more consciously, more purposefully—not to impress the boss or entice a raise or climb some corporate ladder, but simply because it's a good thing to do, for others, for our community, and for ourselves. By not fighting our jobs, by embracing them as allies on our path to spiritual living, we free up considerable energy for personal transformation, for renewing ourselves each day, and discovering more about our place here on planet Earth. Work is a bridge, a classroom, a means *and* an end. As in most of our important personal relationships, it's a place where we can discover more of who we really are, where we forge and are forged.

My goal in writing this book was thus to explore the notion that work itself can provide an ideal classroom for developing our spiritual selves, especially work that features service as a distinguishing characteristic. I also wanted to make the point that society has diminished certain kinds of work for reasons that have a lot more to do with our preoccupation with status and wealth than with the essential value of a job or those who do it.

As we seek to integrate spiritual values into our everyday lives, it becomes increasingly apparent that work must become a part of that process, no matter what kind of work it is. Don't wait for the perfect job or a perfect world; you'll probably be waiting longer than your soul can bear. The place and time to start is where you are now. That's the beauty of working with spirit—it's ready whenever you are ready. And why wait? Your efforts, no matter how tentative, will be richly rewarded. "When a man takes one step toward God, God takes more steps toward that man than there are sands in the worlds of time . . ."

From the boiler room to the boardroom, people still want, *need*, to reinvigorate their work life with purpose, hope, enthusiasm, and service.

Take This Job and Love It can, I hope, recast the potential of work to encompass the larger search for meaning and spiritual satisfaction. But its unique appeal is to go right to the heart of what we do, the myriad tasks and challenges that make up our daily work. It is at this level, in the doing of our jobs and the services that we provide, that one can find the inspiration and the motivation to use work as a tool for personal and spiritual growth. This book is for anyone who believes that who you are, what you do, and how you do it are equal partners in this thing we call work and, ultimately, this thing we call life.

Introduction

When we think of what is meant by the phrase "a spiritual path," the images that take shape more often than not have the feel of something special: solitary walks through a cathedral of redwoods; echoing chants in an ancient monastery; the selfless pursuit of healing and wholeness. We are moved by the spiritual journeys of others, whose tales of struggle, drama, and triumph fill the shelves of bookstores and libraries. Theirs are heroic stories, bigger than life, the stuff of legend and myth and inspiration.

Our stories, by comparison, seem to fall short of such grand tableaus of achievement. The angels, we are certain, flee from the tedious details of our day-to-day routines. Sometimes there's a breakthrough—a coincidence, an intuition—that reminds that there's still mystery in the world, but most of the time it's either soap operas or sitcoms, a head-shaking tale of struggle against the craziness of the world, the frustrations of our jobs, and the failure of our efforts to find reason and comfort in the midst of our frantic lives.

As a result of this chaos, I think that we delude ourselves into thinking that the spiritual path is only for the chosen or the brilliant or shiny-headed monks murmuring mantras of enlightenment at the edge of a distant world. In this "unennobling" of ourselves, however, we may be taking the easy way out: We think of ourselves as merely the dishwasher or the hairstylist or the waiter or the dockworker or the lowest cog in a corporate machine. Our achievements are inconsequential; our aspirations are laughable in their smallness.

Perhaps I exaggerate. Life for most is not such a dismal affair: We are clothed and sheltered. We have food to eat. The television keeps us company if no one else will. It's true, though, that very few of us see ourselves as living a mythic life, one characterized by the play of archetypal forces. Such paths are walked by the "rainmakers" and the paradigm busters, those who have been called or pushed into action. Scholar/philosopher/author Jean Houston, for example, whose childhood was played out on the sets of Hollywood, writes in her memoir *A Mythic Life*, "I have swum in the Ganges . . . planted rice in China . . . danced with lepers in the Congo . . . seen trance dancers in Jogjakarta." Hers has clearly been a path of extraordinary circumstance and opportunity. The rest of us must be satisfied with a holiday in Mexico or a weekend in the woods, all-too-brief interruptions in the drumbeat of our 9-to-5 worlds.

Our lives need not make the headlines or become the subjects of bestsellers in order to be filled with meaning, however. The experiences that have shaped us, both the mundane and the occasionally profound, are every bit as important as any epic achievement when viewed from a broader perspective.

"The mythic quality of my life is by no means unique," Houston writes. "It is only my individual version of the pattern taking place among us all; the local stories of our lives are bound up with the larger story happening the world over. . . . We are becoming vulnerable to our own psychic depths as well as to the realities of other people."

Indeed, only recently have we come to realize that in this giant, crazy thing that we call life, we are more than just forgettable specks whose lives start with a wail and end with an exhausted sigh. Even if we've only been spun out of dust, as some would have us believe, what magical dust that must be, sprinkled as it were on this tiny ball in the midst of an incomprehensibly large universe.

I believe that we are more than this, though—that our lives have a purpose and that there is meaning in everything we do that transcends what appears on the surface. "Are we not all divine? Are we not all made for a higher life?" asked Mother Teresa. If we pay attention, we will indeed notice a longing, maybe just the seed of one, or perhaps a fiery ball in the pits of our stomachs, for a life that honors our deepest feelings of self-worth, that sees in the world around us—including where we work—the potential for goodness and wholeness.

An explosion in sales of books on prayer, faith, and "do-it-yourself" spirituality reflects a powerful surge of interest in affairs of the soul. Phyllis Tickle, a former academic who has become something of an expert on the shifting winds of religion and spirituality in American society, writes in *Re-Discovering the Sacred: Spirituality in America* that "for the [past] thirty years . . . from the dawning of the Age of Aquarius and the crooning of the flower children to the present moment, the introduction of the sacred into everyday conversation and ordinary considerations has been a steady, documentable, direct evolution." A *TV Guide* poll in February 1997 found that 68 percent of the 800-plus people surveyed said that they would like to see more prime-time spirituality on television. Spirituality in this instance was defined as "a belief in a higher being but not necessarily an affiliation with a particular organized religion." *Touched by an Angel*, a show about a heaven-sent trio of divine messengers, led by Della Reese, who act as a kind of Charlie's Angels of the spirit, was an instant hit. Its sudden popularity reflects a thirst for inspiration, for being, well, touched, in a place that is calling out for attention.

When I discussed the focus of this book—about how one's job, no matter what it is, can be part of a spiritual path—with a friend, however, she remarked that "you don't do spirit" in places like offices or restaurants or department stores, to which we could probably add nearly every other establishment that has no overtly religious or "transformative" mission. Most people think that spirituality is so reflective of our deepest, private selves that its expression must be confined to home or church, in the sacred presence of our chosen god or belief system.

What many of us have forgotten—or never realized—is that we are spiritual by definition (at least insofar as the origins of language are concerned). Being spiritual is a fundamental part of our nature that has neither beginning nor end, something that cannot be turned on and off like a faucet. The word *spirit* comes from the Latin *spiritus*, which literally means "breath." It is also akin to the Latin *spirare*, which means to blow or breathe. According to the *American Heritage Dictionary of the English Language*, spirit is "the vital principle or animating force within living beings; incorporeal consciousness." So spirituality, "the quality or state of being spiritual," would suggest that the very act of breathing qualifies us as spiritual beings, at least at the core of who we are.

The latest findings of science are no less compelling, telling us that at the most elemental level of existence we are all made of the same stuff, infinite variations on a single theme. The foundational pulse of creation hums in every form. This is a remarkable conclusion, coming as it does from the summit of rational thinking. So in response to my friend's concern, I say that you can't *not* do spirit. The challenge is to do it consciously.

And how would this look? Practically, such a devotion

would be anchored in values—generosity, honesty, joy, courage, patience, strength, sensitivity, and compassion—and in responding to whatever comes up in life with confidence, caring, and, at times, humility. It is something to be felt, shared, nurtured, and *lived*, not hidden on private altars or saved for Sunday mornings. It would wake us up to an experience of being intimately connected to everything and everyone around us—part of a meaningful whole—and then honoring that sacred web with our thoughts and our actions.

A path, then—in our case, a spiritual path—can be anything that brings us closer to an experience of being spiritual or any road on which the qualities and values presented above are expressed. In the broadest sense, just being alive on this Earth is such a path. In the introduction to his book, *Your Signature Path: Gaining New Perspectives on Life and Work*, Geoffrey M. Bellman writes, "Billions of people have walked the earth. Over five billion of us are here right now . . . cutting our paths through the world. As we make these paths, we create our unique selves. . . . Thousands of people have walked this same ground before us, but we each walk it in our own way. Map our individual paths across the surface of this planet and see the peaks we have attained, the circles in which we have turned, and the well-worn routes we have favored. These are our signature paths."

The labor we do is part of this broader path, another opportunity to make our unique imprint. Unfortunately, it's the last place where we usually expect to find a spiritual dimension. It's often a great hole in the middle of our days—and for many of us, our nights—that's filled with something that we call work; a place more vilified than sanctified, where the budding flowers of our spiritual yearning are often crushed under the weight of our various corporate missions, all having something to do with profits and paychecks. As we become more sensitized to our spiritual needs, however, we begin to realize that it gets harder and harder to ignore those needs inside the boundaries of our work lives.

We can't just shut off this "waking up" process. If it encounters an obstacle, such as eight hours a day of banging one's head against a desk, it will start pushing against it, creating friction and making noise. We can never feel totally whole or at peace if our work life is not part of the transformation. If this is left unresolved, a conflict between our hearts and our pocketbooks begins to form in which our work lives and the rest of our lives appear spiritually incompatible. A kind of schizophrenia is then created in which half of our waking lives is spent as if a part of us didn't exist; we end up shortchanging ourselves on the richness that a full-time spiritual path can offer.

Fortunately, work can be so much more. Work is, in fact, remarkably undervalued as a source of inspiration and a place where we can exercise our nobler intentions. This is no less true for the street sweeper and the shoeshine man than it is for those in any other profession. Indeed, many of the jobs that, by societal decree, are considered lower on the status chart offer fertile ground from which true spirituality can blossom. Devotional expression in our work and in our workplaces has nothing to do with dress codes or salaries or rooms with a view. If spirit and heart are to be found anywhere in the labors of our day, they are present in what each of us brings to those labors.

Irritable customers, greasy fries, and bawling babies are hardly the stuff of angelic choirs. Add to those the million other irritations that characterize our various work lives— unhelpful colleagues, cranky bosses, the pressure of deadlines—and we see a world that only a saint could get through unscathed. Yet, in each instance, each of us has an opportunity to add to the sum total of goodness in the world in the way we conduct ourselves and in the level of sensitivity and heart that we bring to our contact with those around us. It is in the minutiae of our lives, whether at home or at the workplace, that we show that the lessons of spirit have been learned: "Great opportunities to help others seldom come," it has been said, "but small ones surround us daily." A compassionate, even humorous, response to life's challenges is satisfying at the soul level, the only level that really counts, the one that when nurtured always nurtures us back.

Although it is often overlooked, the serving of others can be the sacred ground on which to begin manifesting those qualities of character—love, patience, mindfulness, humility, and strength—that define a spiritual life. Ralph Waldo Emerson wrote, "It is one of the most beautiful compensations of this life that no man can sincerely try to help another without helping himself. . . . Serve and thou shall be served. If you love and serve men, you cannot, by any hiding or stratagem, escape the remuneration."

This book is a celebration of that spirit and an invitation to see in even the simplest and humblest acts the potential for transforming the routines of our work life into blessed moments.

Finding the Way Out

Would that life were like the shadow
cast by a wall or a tree, but it is like
the shadow of a bird in flight.
—*THE TALMUD*

Too often, waiting tables or any other kind of "service" job is looked upon as a temporary stop on the way to more lucrative and socially acceptable positions; a necessary evil; the bottom rung on the ladder to occupational respectability. Even the eminent clergyman and writer Matthew Fox, in his seminal book *The Reinvention of Work*, envisions workplace transformations in such areas as farming, education, psychology, business, science, and so on, but generally overlooks what economists dryly characterize as the service sector.

Yet, according to U.S. Bureau of Labor statistics projecting employment trends to the year 2005, "service-producing jobs will account for the majority of all future job growth. Professional specialty occupations are projected to increase the fastest and to add the most jobs—over 5 million." The study adds that "service workers are expected to add 4.6 million jobs. These two groups—on opposite ends of the educational attainment and earnings spectrum—are expected to provide more than half of the total projected job growth in 1994–2005."

These startling observations raise a couple of interesting issues.

- The transformation of society from a primarily industrial one to one that revolves around information is accentuating the need for and importance of service as a component of our workaday lives.
- "Service workers" continue to be stigmatized as poor and undereducated, thus demeaning their contribution to the economic, social, and spiritual fabric of our collective human experience.

That stigma may be taking its toll. A 1997 Gallup poll found that while 53 percent of all respondents gave high ratings to the quality of U.S. products, only 36 percent gave similar marks to service. Thirty-one percent felt that the quality of the service they receive has been in decline, with employee attitude topping the list of reasons. Is this a reflection of the person or the system? It's probably a little of both.

Where Do We Go from Here?

In our society's version of progress, we are what we have, and we never have enough. The measure of our value comes from dollar signs and acquisitions: the clothes we wear, the cars we drive, the work we do, the houses we live in. The relentless emphasis is on looking good and getting ahead: "He who dies with the most toys wins." Ambition, competition, and the reduction of work into soulless transactions of labor for money have defined the modern workplace. It's no wonder that the world of commerce—at any level—often appears devoid of life. It has become a means to an end, not an end in itself. Even the fashionable notion of "win-win" is somehow incomplete, implying as it does a conditional transaction, an attachment to a measurable outcome. Service as we have come to know it means giving for the purpose of receiving.

When work and spirituality come up in conversation, the discussion frequently gravitates toward sweeping visions of what the office will look and feel like when spiritual principles are integrated. It also veers to the search for—in fact, the *need* to find—"meaningful" work.

Many have written eloquently about such a new world of commerce. The late futurist Willis Harman, for example, in *Creative Work: The Constructive Role of Business in a Transforming Society*, envisioned that "in new paradigm business, people actualize themselves through meaningful, creative work that emphasizes not only economic profit but also social responsibility and ecological awareness. Working in humane workplaces that encourage the expression of higher values, such as humanitarian service and social justice, people use the vehicle of work to bring about personal and collective transformation in society."

There actually *is* a slow renaissance under way in how work is viewed. A growing number of far-sighted leaders are coming to the conclusion that in order to survive and prosper in an increasingly unpredictable world, businesses must incorporate a broader set of values than just conquest and economic growth.

Companies such as Ben & Jerry's, Smith & Hawken, Citizen's Trust, Working Assets, Levi-Strauss, The Body Shop, Aveda, and many others are transforming their work environments with a commitment to meeting their employees' needs beyond just a financial level. Everything from child care and flextime to management teams and community service have turned certain businesses into companies that people are proud to work for, where they feel they are being treated as more than just tools of production. The trust, respect, and loyalty that follows can't usually be purchased by a paycheck alone.

Many of these changes are being driven not by upper management but by those below the top of the corporate pyramid who are no longer satisfied with work as merely a means to pay the rent. They want more from their workplaces; they want to stretch themselves creatively, find meaning in what they do, and go home satisfied rather than drained.

Unfortunately, the number of companies that put their employees' needs ahead of their bankers' is still dwarfed by the number that do not. Deadening monotony and dehumanizing environments still characterize many occupations, making it almost impossible to find one's spiritual center. Indeed, studies have shown that among clerical jobs and those where much of one's time is spent in front of a computer terminal, rates of stress-related disease are significantly higher than those found in other occupations. Such afflictions manifest themselves as everything from indigestion, headaches, and exhaustion to coronary disease, stroke, and mental illness. Factors cited include having to perform monotonous tasks; underutilization of skills; demanding, uncaring management; relentless pacing; and lack of decision-making power.

In a study of British civil servants that tracked nearly 7,400 men and women over a five-year period, researchers concluded that abnormally high incidences of heart disease were found among those individuals who had little decision-making control at their jobs or who did work that was boring and repetitive or did not take full advantage of their skills. Other factors, such as poor health habits or limited access to health insurance, didn't explain the higher incidences. "Our research suggests that illness in the workplace is to some extent a management issue," concluded Michael G. Marmot of the International Centre for Health and Society at University

College in London, who was the lead author of the report. "The way work is organized appears to make an important contribution . . ."

The onset of downsizing and dislocation and the two-income family have only complicated the stresses on those who strive to balance their work lives with their personal lives. Indeed, despite unprecedented economic growth marked by low unemployment and a record-breaking stock market, worker anxieties are high. Seventy percent of all workers surveyed in a nationwide poll in 1997 said that they have less job security now than they had 20 or 30 years ago. Seventy-three percent said there's more on-the-job stress, while 59 percent said that they have to work harder to make a decent living.

Such grim realities raise important and fundamental questions about economic justice, how we treat each other as human beings, and the kinds of values that are really driving our culture's economic engines. These are deep and complicated issues that aren't going away as society accelerates toward the twenty-first century. To be sure, the messages in this book are in no way intended to divert attention from these very real issues. We must do everything we can to create workplaces that support the essential dignity and economic needs of all who are thus engaged. In the famous hierarchy of human motivations developed by American psychologist Abraham Maslow, basic requirements such as food, shelter, safety, and so on must be met before an individual can begin to experience the higher aspirations of love, compassion, knowledge, and ultimately, self-actualization. A full stomach is a much better stimulus of noble action than gnawing hunger. The same goes for the spirit; in situations where basic conditions for experiencing self-esteem are absent, there is little energy to do much more than endure.

It's not surprising, then, that workplace satisfaction, or at least the search for it, is increasingly being found outside of traditional corporate walls. For some, it's a matter of survival as they fall victim to a bean-counter's ax. For others, the choice is deliberate. The result is a surge of newly disposed workers who are using the opportunity to "find themselves" as they seek—or invent—the perfect job. Marsha Sinetar tapped into these new realities some years back with her ground-breaking book, *Do What You Love, The Money Will Follow*. In it, she invited readers to live their dreams of creating work that resonated from their deepest selves: "Each of us must eventually submit to the meaning and purpose of life as we are destined to live it from within ourselves, even when such submission calls for a sacrifice of unfulfilled potential which may seem to us a personal loss or defeat. . . . [Unfortunately] we learn that what we really want is wrong or shameful. This is certainly the case for so many who were taught that they must become 'professional' people or gain a certain credentialed standing in the community but who—deep within themselves—longed for something simpler and less complicated as an occupation."

Her words are still an inspirational call to action, although she wisely cautions those who commit to such a path that the money doesn't always follow right away, nor in the amount that they might expect. "Following your bliss," she suggests, doesn't always mean that your life will be blissful; it will take you where you want to go, but you may not always have fun getting there. It's a good but difficult road.

For many of us, however, it may not be a matter of finding our "true" calling but simply of being called or of doing work that needs to be done for no other reason than that's where we happen to be. We aren't climbing a corporate ladder, we aren't chained to a post in a sweatshop, we're just plain working, which, wrote Studs Terkel in his book *Working*, "is about ulcers as well as accidents, about shouting matches as well as fistfights, about nervous breakdowns as well as kicking the dog around. It is, above all (or beneath all), about daily humiliations. . . . It is about a search, too, for daily meaning as well as daily bread, for recognition as well as cash, for astonishment rather than torpor; in short, for a sort of life rather than a Monday through Friday sort of dying."

Terkel goes on to talk about the rare few who "find a savor in their daily job": the piano tuner seeking the perfect sound, the bookbinder who's saving a piece of history, or the stonemason who appreciates a job well-done. But for most, he says, work is a chore, drudgery, an affront to one's dignity, the final battleground where men and women confront the cold-blooded machine of commerce and the thoughtlessness of their fellow humans.

In Service to the Whole

So where does this leave us? Is bitter resignation our only recourse? Do we submerge our dreams under a deluge of "happy hour" cocktails and pray that Monday never comes? That's a heck of a way to live.

There is another option, and that is to recognize that work—no matter what kind—is ripe with opportunity for exploring and developing our spiritual selves. Instead of thunderbolts of career-path illumination, maybe the idea of a calling has more to do with being aware of what our daily tasks are asking of us. Indeed, the personal growth that Sinetar refers to when we commit to a "right livelihood" is no less available to those who consciously apply themselves to what they are doing, whatever it may be; the same challenges and opportunities are present. In other words, "bliss" can be experienced right where you are right now, even if your employer graduated from the troglodyte school of management or your job description never lights up the pages of *Business Week* or *Forbes*. In the fashionable struggle to strive for a better life, we've ignored the fact that what we are doing *today* has value, even something as basic as hauling trash, delivering mail, working a cash register, or answering phones.

It's fine, of course, to aspire to new challenges and successes, to envision work that resonates with our highest aspirations. But these aspirations are only distractions if they continually draw us away from the present moment, from the maxim that reminds us, "Before enlightenment, chop wood, carry water. After enlightenment, chop wood, carry water." In a world in which "getting ahead" means bigger, stronger, faster, it's easy to forget that every act of labor is a potentially sacred one. A gray suit and leather briefcase don't necessarily bring us closer to God; acts as simple as washing a shirt or shining a shoe or giving a manicure can be more than enough. Indeed, in the sometimes rough patchwork that is community, such work is the invisible glue that keeps the whole in place.

In Hermann Hesse's book *The Journey to the East*, Hesse fictionalizes an assortment of accomplished characters—Don Quixote, Siddhartha, Demian, and others—who are on a collective pilgrimage of spiritual intent as members of what he calls the League. Among them is a man named Leo the Server, whom Hesse describes as "one of our servants. . . . He helped to carry the luggage and was often assigned to the personal service of the Speaker. This unaffected man had something so pleasing, so unobtrusively winning about him, that everyone loved him. He did his work gaily, usually sang or whistled as he went along, was never seen except when needed—in fact, an ideal servant."

Despite the obvious capabilities of the group's members, however, they fall into disarray when Leo inexplicably disappears several months into the journey. "On that cool autumn morning when it was discovered that our servant Leo was missing and that all search for him remained fruitless," Hesse writes, "I was certainly not the only one who, for the first time, had a feeling of impending disaster and menacing destiny."

And later: "Hardly had Leo left us, when faith and concord amongst us was at an end; it was as if the life-blood of our group flowed away from an invisible wound." Indeed, the group never recovers, and many if its members wander off in confusion and despair.

The story conveys the sometimes imperceptible yet essential contribution made by those who take service to its highest level of display. In the case of Leo (who turned out to be not just the servant but the actual leader of the League), he was serving not only those in his immediate presence but also a higher purpose: spirit. For he knew, in the words of a student of Hesse's work, that to place the needs of one's ego above those of the greater community is to court suffering; the willingness to serve is the key to bliss. "Thus Leo, as the incarnation of the League and its Superior, is at the same time its most devoted servant. His smile is the smile of ironic renunciation, for he knows that mastery in the everyday world is illusory while service to the timeless spirit is eternal."

One man who raised service to an art form was Isaac Bassett. Appointed as a Senate page at the age of 12 by Senator Daniel Webster in 1831, Bassett was eventually promoted to messenger in 1838, and 23 years later was named assistant doorkeeper, a post he held until his death in 1895. He was an astute chronicler of Senate life, and his diary entries offer a fascinating glimpse into the personalities and the dramas that marked nineteenth-century American politics.

With few complaints and seldom a missed day, he worked under the same roof for 64 years. While it's true that his duties were performed for a venerable institution, adding a dimension to his work that few others could claim, the tasks themselves might be considered menial. As a page and messenger, for example, Bassett ran errands, delivered mail, filed paperwork, and licked envelopes, among other chores, until he was past 40. Few of us would have stayed so committed.

His motto, "I always [make] it a rule never to be in a senator's way," so impressed his employers that they elevated him to assistant doorkeeper. In that position, his duties changed somewhat—assigning seats, "stopping" the clock (to avoid inconvenient deadlines), relaying messages from infirm senators, and replenishing the Honorable Orville Browning's tumbler with a bit of gin from time to time. He was there to ensure that the needs of the senators were met.

So moved were Senate members by Bassett's reliability and unwavering loyalty over the years that they would honor him from time to time, most notably in 1881 with "a gold-lined snuff box of beaten silver" from Tiffany's that commemorated his 50 years of service "as an officer of [the United States Senate], in recognition of his personal worth and official fidelity." A plaque on the wall of the Capitol building says of this "Venerable Doorkeeper" that "he became for many a symbol, the last tangible reminder of the Senate's earlier, great days."

This notion of service as a vital part of the workplace is gaining converts. Not a month goes by, it seems, without a book on leadership coming out, extolling the virtues of service to eager corporate managers looking for new motivational tools. Craig Neal of the Heartland Institute, an organization devoted to bringing spirituality into the workplace, sees service as playing a pivotal role in how people are perceiving a more meaningful relationship with their work. "When people feel they are being of service to something larger than themselves, then something happens—an alchemy—that transcends logical thought and possibilities; the undoable gets done, the impossible is possible," he says.

This is the kind of breakthrough thinking that is needed right now: seeing in our work the chance to serve—not just the person in front of us or on the other end of the phone (which is certainly important enough) but also the greater whole, that of which we are a part in countless ways. It is through this door that we can begin to find the inspiration to bring an entirely new attitude to our jobs. We aren't just getting our paychecks or filling time or performing our duties as good members of society; we are actually in touch with the idea that we can have a meaningful impact in the world. There are many ways in which our work can touch someone and transform us in the process. When we see this potential, it is easier to make work a part of our spiritual path. The knowledge begins to ground our experience of work and help us perceive its value outside of material measures. Companies may change, jobs may change, and careers may change, but the recognition that in our work lies the means of spiritual attainment is something precious that we can take wherever we go.

Of Lemons
and Lemonade

*The basic difference between an ordinary
man and a warrior is that a warrior takes
everything as a challenge, while an ordinary
unaware man takes everything as either a
blessing or a curse.*

—*THE SORCERER DON JUAN TO HIS STUDENT,
CARLOS CASTANEDA*

According to the National Restaurant Association, there are nearly 800,000 dining locations in the United States employing 9.5 million people—8 percent of the total work-force—and generating $320 billion per year. Almost 50 billion meals were eaten in restaurants during 1995; on a typical day, almost half of all adults had a meal in a restaurant.

The rituals of eating in this country are as varied as its citizens, multiplied by the various forms that dining out has taken and the times of day at which we eat. Breakfast is different from lunch is different from dinner; fast food is different from pub food is different from the fare at a four-star steak house. What is common to all of these experiences, however, is not just that food is eaten but that it is served. It may involve no more than taking an order over a counter, but in every case, contact is being made and energy exchanged.

A National Restaurant Association survey concluded that "after good food, service is the most important component of a pleasant dining experience." Indeed, the play of forces at work in the simple act of serving food contains all of the elements for journeying a sacred path. One is forever challenged to be patient, kind, sensitive, attentive, clear, nurturing, and humble, all of which can lead to greater self-knowledge and wisdom. What greater challenge can there be than to remain dignified when insulted, cheerful when stiffed or ignored, or calm when confronted with chaos?

Despite the fact that millions of people have done, will do, or are still doing this kind of work, however, the serving of food is often something that is only endured by those who do it, a dance of tension involving overheated cooks, money-conscious managers, and demanding customers, an endless series of simple and often thoughtless transactions: service for money, money for food, food for survival.

Given such a dreary image, it's no wonder that waiting tables has often been relegated to a grimly amusing career footnote or a destination of inferior class; dismissed as a subculture of marginality peopled by students, single mothers, misfits, and never-wills; characterized as a means to an end until a "real life" shows up. "I became a waitress because I needed the money fast, and you don't get it in an office," says Dolores in Studs Terkel's *Working*. "My husband and I broke up; he left me with debts and three children. My baby was six months old."

The pressures *not* to be your best—a frantic pace, insensitive customers, routine, routine, routine—are difficult to resist. The gripes of waitpeople are legendary. The following are from a list that I found on the Internet.

- Customers who act as if waiting on tables is easy. A waitperson needs legs of iron, a memory like a steel trap, and the patience of a saint.
- People who ask obscure and irrelevant questions such as, "Are your cows fed with wheat grass or crabgrass?" then wince with disapproval, slump in their chairs, and slowly reconsider their menus if the answer is not what they hoped. And then there are always those people who want to concoct entirely new meals by merging the best of three or four different entrées into something just for them.
- Complaints that the restaurant doesn't have what a customer wants, as if it were possible for the servers to cook the meals themselves. The servers don't design the menus.
- Patrons who order a dish that they don't understand but never thought to ask about, then complain when it arrives.
- During busy shifts, people who order a cup of coffee and three refills and then read the newspaper for an hour. This situation creates a great deal of stress for servers because there's nothing they can say, but they still have to endure the nasty stares of the people who are waiting to sit down.
- Folks who announce that they don't believe in tipping—after they've finished eating.
- Large parties that ask for separate checks when one has already been written.
- Pranksters who insist that they really did find a belt buckle in their soup; such jokes are hardly ever funny to a waiter or waitress.

And thus the dark side of dining out is exposed, at least from the server's point of view. Every occupation has its shadows. What cab driver hasn't experienced the same kind of disregard? What store clerk hasn't felt as if people couldn't care less if he lived or died? What telephone operator hasn't been treated like the machine she has struggled not to become? It's easy to become dispirited when our work isn't valued by society or when we ourselves don't value it, when our interactions with others seem rote, lifeless, or even antagonistic. At such times, what motivation is there to consider our situation in any light other than "I've got to get out of this place"?

If we do choose to shift our perspective, however, a true transformation can begin to take place: in ourselves, in the work we do, and ultimately, in the world we live in. More than likely, these initial steps into consciousness will take place at the "mundane" level of our daily work lives—in the doing of our tasks and the mindfulness we bring to them— where the seeds of spirit are often planted. With such an awareness, the challenge to be our best—mentally, emotionally, and spiritually—is always present, giving us countless opportunities to experience our work as we never have before. Waiting tables, or any job that is long on service and short on glamour, can be a life-affirming adventure and a means to a spiritual end, a place to discover—and inspire—dignity and wholeness, where one can be part of the solution, not the problem. "What we do" transforms into a place where "who we are" can blossom and mature in a deeply satisfying way. Ultimately, the impetus for change has to come from inside. When our work doesn't give us what we need, we need to bring more to it. Observation, research, and personal experience have taught me that the more difficult the situation, the more imperative this is.

Gambling on Attitude

In the late seventies, I quit graduate school in Reno to become a full-time croupier and blackjack dealer. The local casinos presented a seductive alternative to the tedium of academic life: good money, flexible hours, and high entertainment value. And for a while, it felt like the most exciting thing I had ever done, every bit as interesting as the movie images made it seem.

Over time, however, it started to wear me down: the noise, the smoke, the monotony, the people. By the third or fourth year, I had become paralyzed with disenchantment, hyperventilating my anxiety to psych myself up for my shift.

As I struggled with this sorry mess, I happened to meet a woman who for a time distracted me from my troubles. But the distraction was short-lived; I just couldn't escape from my unhappiness. After hearing a few too many complaints about my dealing discontent, she challenged me to change my experience, saying, in effect, "Don't blame everyone else for your troubles; you're the one choosing to react as you do. Make different choices."

At first, unwilling to acknowledge that I had any control over my situation, I thought that she was giving me some kind of New Age line. But with no other options and realizing that I had nothing to lose, I decided to give it a try. I stopped hyperventilating and learned to walk into the club with a different attitude. I took things less personally and trained myself not to go into negative spaces when the throb of the club threatened to engulf me. I tried to just "be myself" and found, after a surprisingly short time, that my experience was changing. I wasn't so exhausted at the end of the night, and my shift miraculously went faster. The noise didn't seem as maddening, I was much more tolerant of the people at my table—even the alcohol-challenged—and I rediscovered the word *amusement* (as in pleasing, not park).

I can't say that I had transformed the flipping of cards into a performance of Zen-like harmony, but I had enough breakthroughs to really start turning things around, so much so that I could actually visualize never leaving my job; I could see myself flipping plastic and calling out numbers until my hair thinned and my teeth fell out. Interestingly, only a month or two later, an opportunity to leave the club presented itself, and I knew that I had been released. But the irony is that by then it almost didn't matter.

Here's to the Weekday Warriors

For a time, I was a great fan of Carlos Castaneda, who in the late 1960s and early 1970s wrote a series of best-selling books based on his alleged relationship with Don Juan Matus, a Toltec sorcerer who lived in northwestern Mexico. As a result of this relationship, which spanned a number of years, Castaneda himself—according to his writings—emerged as a shaman capable of tremendous feats, and he became an idol of sorts for many like me in the impressionable years of our youth. A bit of an eccentric, his growing reclusiveness only added to the power of his legend, until any story at all of his whereabouts was elevated to a sacred script. I recall one in particular that said that his last known location was a small Southwestern town, where he worked in the kitchen of an old diner. I was stunned. A diner? The great Carlos Castaneda? I later read a rare interview with him in which he stated that he purposely chose such work to maintain his humility and honor the way of the warrior to which he had committed.

The idea of warriorhood is an interesting one. Historically, the great warriors—real and imagined—fought on battlefields against tangible and bigger-than-life enemies. Their sole purpose was to confront overwhelming odds in order to uphold justice, protect the innocent, and occasionally win the beautiful maiden's hand. Their exploits were immortalized—giant-killer David, Joan of Arc, Odysseus, Don Quixote, the Green Berets, the Knights of the Round Table. They were gladiators of the spirit and defenders of all that was virtuous and good.

The warrior image still lives today, most obviously on the silver screen; our movies are filled with images of people like you and me who either choose or are called to engage in a fight for their lives. Importantly, however, it's not always a physical life that's at stake. Indeed, the opponents are as likely to be found inside our favorite heroes and heroines as outside them. Luke Skywalker, for example, had to learn to trust in the spiritual wisdom of "The Force" before vanquishing his final foe; Ralph Macchio's Karate Kid had to confront his lack of faith in himself. What relevance do such episodic fairy tales have to the butcher, the baker, and the candlestick maker? They are blown-up images of the forces at work in all of our lives, touching us in the places where we clutch our most private—and noble—aspirations.

The qualities of warriorship—courage, bravery, integrity, honesty, steadfastness, honor, and so on—have as much relevance today as they ever had during the myth-rich times of bloodthirsty warlords and thundering gods. The most obvious threats to our safety and livelihood have diminished, but there is no shortage of challenges, many of which can be found inside our hearts and minds, within the matrix of our psychological and emotional programming. We must confront not packs of wild animals or gun-toting desperadoes but inertias of the spirit: fear, frustration, lethargy, despair, and routine. They have always been with us, of course, but as the need for wholeness asserts itself, these cries for help seem somehow louder, calling us in the quieter moments of our days when the noise of modern life isn't filling all the empty spaces.

Many of these self-defeating patterns are generated—or at least reinforced—at work. If we are to live spiritual lives, however, work must become an integral part of that path. Seeing our workplaces and our jobs as vehicles for spiritual growth requires looking at them with new eyes and seeing that below the surface, there is a wealth of opportunity to be mined.

Everyone is familiar with the concept of the weekend warrior: pickup games at the local gym, afternoon softball, stretching the usual three-mile run to five. We push our bodies as far as our fitness and desire allow. We know that we'll never quite recapture the vigor and potency of our youth, but we embrace the challenge anyway, and in so doing, we connect with a part of ourselves that rejoices in the effort no matter the skill level. And the challenge is not just physical, for in the doing of it we find opportunities for stretching our mental, emotional, and even spiritual muscles by playing fair, honoring our bodies, respecting our competitors, embracing companionship, and perhaps most important, exercising our ability to keep things in perspective. This is especially important when the ego is engaged, for if our weekend sweats serve no better purpose than to act as an homage to vanity or a test of endurance or a chance to make someone eat dirt, the results can actually be destructive, keeping us stuck in old patterns. When, on the other hand, we give the best of ourselves—without conditions, from the heart—we walk away feeling refreshed and renewed.

We can apply this same spirit at work as *weekday* warriors, pushing ourselves to do the best we can in a way that is similarly nourishing to body and soul. The challenge is to first embrace what we do as important and valuable—to re-view our work—and then to begin changing our relationship to it, to see our jobs as working for our best interests and helping us to:

• Bring the spirit of service into everything we do
• Take pride in what we do, and in so doing feel good about who we are

- Be more loving and compassionate in our actions toward others
- Be more conscious—more mindful—of what is going on around us
- See that in every interaction with another person lies an opportunity to touch their lives in a positive way

Part of the process involves choice, recognizing that we can choose to have a different experience. Pressure on the job is something quite familiar to most of us. Imagine having to answer calls when all four lines of your telephone stay lit for three solid hours or preparing at the last minute to welcome a busload of tourists at an inconvenient time or coping with more than one manager bearing down on you to meet a sudden deadline. Being of service is much easier when demands are low, but pressure can put our brains in overdrive, make long tempers short, and fill our "space" with anxiety and fear. No one is immune to it, and few jobs are safe from it. How we handle pressure will reflect back to us where our strengths are, as well as our weaknesses. But if we approach it as a lesson, dealing with pressure can teach us to be clear and grounded.

Debra was a waitress at one of the busiest cafés in New York. It was an indoor/outdoor Mexican place, famous for its food and margaritas. Starting at lunch and continuing through dinner, there was always a huge line of eager customers. Each waitress was responsible for 10 tables, which is manageable when parties come and go randomly as they normally do in a restaurant. One night, however, all 10 of Debra's tables became free and then filled up at the same time. This is probably not unlike having 20 relatives—not 6, as planned—show up on your doorstep one Sunday afternoon expecting to be fed— *now*. What did Debra do? Well, she panicked, of course, at least at first.

"Help me," she recalls pleading with the bartender as images of calamity started piling up. "This is not life and death," he reminded her. "It's only food and drinks."

Debra took a moment to catch her breath and put things in perspective. There was nothing to do, she finally decided, other than just be totally honest about what she was feeling and let the chips fall where they may. She went back out to her station and shared with her customers just how difficult and unusual her position was, asking for their support, and adding, "I'm going to do the best I can." The result? They gave her a round of applause! And it turned out to be one of her biggest tip nights of the year. In choosing to release her fears and simply surrender to her situation, she allowed a "solution" (to take it as it came) to emerge that honored her as well as her customers.

Science of Mind founder Ernest Holmes said, "We cannot lead a choiceless life. Every day, every moment, every second, there is a choice. If it were not so, we would not be individuals . . ." In the casino, accepting that I had control over my reactions was the real challenge. I had to overcome my attachment to helplessness, to stop justifying my bad attitude with lame excuses for my misery. It was much easier to cede my destiny to other forces, to deny my power to change. But all it really took to start on another road was to adjust my perspective, even slightly, and then use that shift to start making different choices.

Honoring Our Own Story

We each make a unique imprint on the surface of life. Growing up human, we've been through dozens of initiations and felt the joys and sorrows of any saint or master. Each of us has a story worth telling, a story that has meaning and "mythic" dimensions. The "hero's journey" is a road that is open to all of us at any time in our lives—not just Nobel Prize winners or military commandos, but anyone who gets up in the morning and faces the formidable task of surviving in a world that often seems determined to make life miserable. In an interview, storyteller Antoinette Botsford commented that it's really the simple routines in our daily affairs that make up the greater part of spiritual living.

"Many of the stories I tell make a point that the status quo, the stuff of daily life like raising kids or pulling weeds or baking bread, done cheerfully and with a smile at one's lips, is the model for spiritual empowerment," she says. "By far the greatest part of anyone's day is doing simple things consciously and well.

"In most storytelling traditions," she explains, "life is understood as a voyage to self-understanding, with plenty of obstructions and distractions along the way. We are heroes when we choose compassion instead of judgment, generosity instead of greed, kind speech instead of slander, a smile in place of a frown. There is no end to the journey, but in each life there are segments of great challenges to be overcome, whether at the workplace, at home, or elsewhere. How we deal with those challenges—most of which are surely lacking in glamour— constitutes heroism."

In reality, however, squeezed by financial, emotional, and other pressures, it's easy to just give up, to go on autopilot, to make the routines of our workday lifeless and rote. We don't see our lives as having heroic potential, or even as worth a good story. Lacking such a vision, we are blind to the opportunities around us, preferring to have our heroes swashbuckling on-screen or coming to life in the pages of a good novel.

As Daniel Taylor writes in *The Healing Power of Stories*, however, "Our greatest desire, greater even than the desire for happiness, is that our lives mean something. . . . Nothing makes us want to live more than the feeling that we have something important to do. Nothing makes us seem as worthless as the feeling that we do not. Seeing our lives as a story interacting with other stories gives us that sense of being part of a sequence of meaningful events that lead to a significant conclusion."

Our work is part of our story, part of our myth, part of the numinous collective that encompasses all of human experience. It's a place for self-expression and self-reflection and for learning about this spaceship we call Earth. In the thicket of the chaos that confronts us every day in our jobs, there are gifts of the spirit awaiting at every turn, hidden gold in the seeming scrap metal of our daily routines. Our job is to find that gold and use it to enrich our lives. For anyone who seeks to turn their life into a quest for spiritual fulfillment, there is no better place to start than where you work.

The Spiritual Dimensions of Work

It is easy to be friendly to one's friends.
But to befriend the one who regards himself
as your enemy is the quintessence of true
religion. The other is merely business.
—MAHATMA GANDHI

The typical workday is crammed with irritations, beginning with the alarm clock and ending with bumper-to-bumper escape. In between, there is an infinite variety of challenges that we endure, ignore, or bristle or fume at but rarely use for spiritual exercise. This is what makes the workplace something special, though; like our primary relationships, it's an excellent laboratory for exploring who we are, which is always more interesting when things aren't going the way we'd like.

Especially among service jobs, where the needs of others are usually placed ahead of our own, every minute can provide an opening to make choices about the kinds of people we want to be and how we want to contribute to the communities in which we live. Even in the world of bits and bytes, of workers with their eyes glued to computer screens composing images and words, sometimes in a vacuum of human contact, the spiritual pulse beats. The opportunities for such growth may seem less frequent as time disappears into an infinite digital universe, and I believe that technology will never replace flesh and blood as the medium through which we form our self-identity and our relationship to the source of life. But no workplace is immune to the forces of soul-level change.

There will be no end to the journey and the challenge of transforming an eight-hour headache into a worthwhile pursuit of wisdom. In using our workplaces as stimuli to spiritual growth, we will find plenty of opportunities among the people we come in contact with, the details of the actual work, and the roadblocks we stumble into as we learn to accept that where we are is just where we need to be.

Recognize Your Teachers

It's the rare occupation that doesn't revolve around the contact of one human being with another, whether that connection is with fellow employees, the people served, or those whose services are needed to do our jobs. Indeed, our psychological universe consists largely of the contacts that we make with other people, countless interactions that make up a connective web of psychic space. Such interactions can be life-affirming or life-demeaning, profoundly affecting our quality of life—how we feel about who we are and what we're doing. Like monkeys, we often mirror each other: If someone engages you with a high level of integrity and compassion, you're likely to respond in the same spirit. If, on the other hand, you meet a snarling beast, you're likely to snarl back. The sum total of these exchanges, on a scale from satisfying down to life-draining, defines the quality of our days, the directions of our lives, and ultimately, the maturity of our communities and cultures. The result of each interaction is like a stone dropped in a pond of consciousness: Will the ripples be smooth and gentle or turbulent and unsettling?

I once attended a publishing convention in Chicago and stayed at a classy (at least for me) hotel in the center of busy downtown. The place was swarming with guests and staff people: bellhops, doormen, desk clerks, and managers. All week long, I dealt with one or another for room service, to carry bags, to take a message, or to hail a cab. Most of the time, they did what they had to do, reasonably cheerfully or at least without insult, but two people really stood out.

The first was a lanky young man who staffed the luggage waiting room. It was midmorning, and I was nervously pacing the sidewalk where the shuttle vans were unloading and loading passengers. I was there to get a package for a meeting for which, of course, I was late. The young man, juggling one request and then another, striding to and fro on his long legs, nevertheless stood rapt in front of me when I urgently pleaded my case. The entire scene—the rumbling cabs, the *thunking* doors, the voices and the buzz that are always hovering at a hotel's front door—suddenly froze as he absorbed my predicament, totally in the moment, as if nothing else were going on.

"You stay right there," he commanded. He loped off through a door and returned a few minutes later with my package and a big smile on his face. A bellhop? The guy was a Buddha, the pure embodiment of joyful service. It was impossible for me to see him as anything other than a saint, someone to be honored and respected. He elevated my spirit just by being who he was.

The other surprise was Jaeck, the Polish waiter who served breakfast to me and my co-worker on the morning of our departure. Jaeck spoke five different languages—"English is my fifth," he informed us with a wink—and could have rivaled many professionals with his comedic skills and timing. He gleefully entertained us while serving omelets and toast, not so invasively as to make us cower over our coffee but enough to say, "Hey, wake up! A glorious new day has just begun!" We walked out of the restaurant marveling at his extraordinary attitude.

Not everyone manifests "spirit" like this, of course; there are an infinite number of ways to feel connected to who you are and to everyone and everything that is around you, ways that are unique to each individual. Indeed, I'd wager that neither of these two people would actually characterize what they did as being spiritual in nature. They were just "being themselves," but in so doing, they exuded a contagious sense of joy and balance that can only be the result of connecting with something larger than the petty grievances that keep most of us from feeling fully alive. Work was a dance for them, expressed in such simple values as caring, generosity, attentiveness, service, and fun. They made authentic contact—nothing was rote or routine. Their originality showed; they did not hold themselves back.

Our world desperately needs this kind of energy, these sparks of life. They provide the necessary balance to the dehumanizing impact of our mass-market, technology-driven, "I need it yesterday" workplaces. In those professions where service is the prevailing characteristic, the ability to deliver such a gift is truly priceless, leaving a trail of good feeling that can extend in many directions. The result may not always show up on a corporate balance sheet—at least not in a way that is easily apparent—but on the soul's balance sheet, you would find plenty of entries. Such is the challenge—and opportunity— that faces those whose work brings them into frequent contact with others.

Unfortunately, it's easy to forget that in the course of performing our various responsibilities, we are dealing with real people, individuals with their own inner worlds of complex emotions and life experience. In transforming our jobs from drudgery to sacred ground, however, we must begin to acknowledge the essential humanity and goodness in everyone we come in contact with, *no matter what they may be presenting us*. It's easy to be attentive when the people you're dealing with are kind and respectful. But what if they aren't? What if the person scowling in front of you or shouting on the other end of the phone is the last one on earth you'd choose to share an elevator with?

We can never really know what people are bringing with them to interactions. Maybe they've just been fired or lost a beloved pet. No matter where they've been or where they're going, however, they are reaching out to you in that moment because you have something they need or want: directions, a hamburger, a letter, the right computer. They are asking for help, for something that only you can provide. You thus have the power to please or perturb, to serve or impede, to affect the flow of energy and events beyond what you may believe is possible. What an opportunity! How will you use it?

Thankfully, most of the people we come in contact with in our workaday worlds are pleasant enough, which should make the job of compassionate interaction that much easier. But as we shall see later, how we respond depends a lot on how we're feeling about who we are and what we're doing. Do we feel good about ourselves and our work? Do we embrace our roles as servers, seeing in them opportunities to give of ourselves and in so doing (in one of those wonderful paradoxes), get filled up in the process? Or do we "do unto others as we would have others *not* do unto us" because we've forgotten that our lives have meaning, our work has value, and our purpose for being alive is to realize that every moment counts? We must continually ask such questions as we seek in our work the tools for spiritual living.

Green Grass Is Where You Stand

In 1987, Michael Douglas won the Oscar for Best Actor for his role in the movie *Wall Street*. In it, he played Gordon Gecko, a high-stakes, ball-busting, take-no-prisoners deal-maker who is the envy of young, ambitious stockbroker Bud Fox, played by Charlie Sheen. Fox ("I want to be on the other end of this phone," he grimaces after a depressing day of cold-calling potential new clients) sees Gecko as his ticket out of the blue-collar predictability epitomized by his working-class father, played by Martin Sheen.

Unlike the elder Fox, Gecko seems to have it all—wealth, power, women, and control—and he intoxicates Bud with the sweet scent of success. Bud willingly sells his soul to the Mephistophelian Gecko and embarks on a path that he thinks will bring him everything that he's ever dreamed of. Deeper and deeper he falls as he climbs the financial ladder, filling his life with trophies of conquest but filling his soul with nothing. Slowly, inexorably, he gives himself away, finally playing the pawn in Gecko's cold-blooded power play that will put his father out of business. This is Bud's wake-up call, and in dramatic Hollywood fashion, he sees the error of his ways and the goodness of his father's world, and he bests his heartless mentor.

Bud's dilemma has been my dilemma and that of many others: looking elsewhere for satisfaction when all the answers we ever wanted are probably staring us in the face. We are filled with images of what life could—and should—be like, often comparing those images with the pictures we have of our own lives and coming up wanting. There's nothing particularly unusual about this; like crows, we humans are attracted to things that sparkle in the light. Unfortunately, the sparkle is sometimes no deeper than the surface.

I remember a story that was told to me by a doctor from

Thailand whom I met while traveling in Europe. This doctor, a sweet, kind man with a big heart and a gentle smile, was sadly recalling a time during which visitors from a foreign corporation showed up in a number of villages where he was the attending physician. They brought televisions with them and demonstrated these magic boxes to the wide-eyed villagers, who had only known the life of country peasants. Needless to say, they were mesmerized by the fantastic images.

Unfortunately, they didn't have any money, certainly not enough to buy such wonderful devices, but the men from out of town had a solution: The villagers could have their televisions if they just signed a piece of paper. This seemed easy enough, and so the transactions took place, the villages were wired up, and time passed. After a while, the strangers returned to take the televisions back.

"No, no, you can't have them," the villagers cried.

"But you signed this document," the men responded with authority, showing them the piece of paper. The villagers were stricken: What were they to do?

"Well, there is another option," the men from outside explained. "As it's written in this paper, you can keep your televisions if you give us your land."

"Our land?" the villagers clamored. They met and they argued, weighing the value of the land against the value of the televisions. They finally came to a decision: Go ahead, take the land, but leave us our televisions. And so the men claimed much of the land that the villagers had lived on for generations—but no longer valued—and the landscape of that part of Thailand was soon altered forever.

Misplaced values. We tend to attach too much importance to things that don't have lasting consequence while underappreciating or overlooking those that do. That's because in a society that elevates prestige and material gain to religious status, we grow up thinking that anything else is somehow tainted or inadequate. Such a perception is exaggerated by the competitive urgencies that still characterize our capitalistic model; it's usually you against the other guy—or the company down the road or the one across the sea. We thus learn early in life that it's important to get—and stay—ahead and that there's no such a thing as "enough." Consequently, we are rarely satisfied; there's always one more rung on the ladder, one more dollar to be made, one more mile to be run, or one more threat to be vanquished, in an endless circle of unquenched desire. Envy, ambition, longing, and fear have become the engines behind many of our actions. There are those who have and those who have not, and we know which one is preferable.

When we scratch below the surface of money, status, and power, however, we find a whole unexplored world of consequence and challenge that can feed our souls in a way that fame and fortune cannot. Indeed, those are often distractions from the deeper purposes in life, such as acting with compassion, learning the value of humility, and being mindful in how we interact with others. Against the blizzard of images telling us what kind of work is cool and what kind is not, we must hold our ground and appreciate what we have on our plates, for in the simplest of acts lies the heart of what it means to be human.

To discover these riches, we must stop associating certain kinds of work with success, or better yet, start using different yardsticks, such as whether or not we are happy at what we're doing, to measure what we would call the good life. We need to stop identifying too strongly with society's standards of what constitutes valuable work; *all* work is valuable if it needs to be done, and a strong case could be made that it's more important to have our garbage picked up than to have 12 different kinds of detergent to choose from, especially if it's being picked up by the guys in the following story (from an as-yet unpublished book).

The noise of a garbage truck woke me from my wistful musings, and I watched two men, both in early adulthood, pick up the cans and empty them into the truck. Only these guys didn't act like the ones who've been hauling garbage since before The Fall. They did not have the grunt-and-shuffle blues in their faces; they did not walk purposefully and efficiently, anticipating hours of what at least I'd expect was drudgery. In fact, these guys didn't walk at all—I think that's what I noticed first—they danced. They leapt between the cans, the hedges, the driveways, the wild bougainvillea, like an audition for a ballet troupe. One guy would arc a can to the other, who, almost like a trapeze artist, would grab it and swing it into the truck. Then, in an almost un-broken move, he'd swing it back to the first, who'd drop it and then pirouette to the next can. . . . It was graceful, it appeared effortless, it seemed like a game. They were having, well, fun . . . dancing with the cans . . . turning what would be for many just a job into something that seemed very different.

Contrary to what our minds would like to have us believe, the grass is not always greener on the other side, and whether it is or it isn't, we're on *this* side, and we need to attend to that. It is only when we truly accept—and even embrace—the cir-cumstances of our "now" life that our experience of it starts to shift. We all need to make money, of course, and oftentimes the decision of where to work is primarily an economic one. But usually there are other motivations, and it's important to remember what some of those reasons were—those that had nothing to do with money or convenience or other tactical considerations. A house painter, for example, may see beauty in a finished project; a store clerk may enjoy the give-and-take he has with customers and the sharing—however brief—of the stories of the day; a postal worker may thrive in the outdoors despite the occasional canine intervention.

"Sometimes," writes Victoria Moran in *Shelter for the Spirit: How to Make Your Home a Haven in a Hectic World,* "I still whine about chores. Cleaning is boring, repetitive, mindless, unappreciated, physically demanding, sexually stereotyped, and societally undervalued. In this state of boredom, repetition, and mindlessness, however, we can be receptive to the divinity within us. Similarly, being called to an activity that is demanding, stereotyped, and undervalued can be used as an opportunity to gain humility. It can bring us face-to-face with the mystics' paradox: We are dust and we are divine. That's a lot to get from a sponge and a bucket."

For Moran, it's a sponge and a bucket; for others, it may be a steering wheel and a change box, an apron and a tray, or a deck of cards and a comfortable pair of shoes. Such can be the tools of enlightenment, if we allow them.

Becoming a Somebody

The pattern in our society that equates who one is with what they do, when much of what we do isn't valued by that same society, is a pernicious kind of Catch-22. How many times have you been asked "So, what do you do?" and felt a quiver of tentativeness—or a surge of ego—inside? We have become very sensitized to what our work says about who we are—not just what is says to us but what it says to others, who, however unwittingly, may place various types of occupations on a hierarchy of social or economic status. It means that many jobs are never given a chance; based on a dominant perception, they're tainted by their very nature. The effects of such typecasting can be devastating, emotionally and psychologically, as we grapple with the realization that what we do is somehow less in the eyes of others.

If we weren't so dependent on outside approval, those judgments would have little effect. But we are dependent; we do rely on such acceptance to validate who we are. The mechanisms behind this are complicated and deep. They involve how we were raised and the impact of "conditional loving"; how the economic paradigm of Western culture favors material gain and intellectual agility; how winning and losing are the dominant idioms of success and failure; and much, much more. While we shouldn't ignore the various architectures (social, moral, and so on) of our communities, it seems that "self-worth" has a lot less to do with the actual self than with how others regard and respect that self. Vulnerable to the whims and wrong-mindedness of a value-dysfunctional world, it's thus no wonder that our self-esteem is greatly influenced by how we perceive our work and how others perceive it.

James M. Childs Jr., in his book *Ethics in Business: Faith at Work*, talks about the difference between a "nobody" and a "somebody": "In our work life, we are especially prone to linking self-worth to generally accepted indicators of success. If we are doing well on the job and getting recognized for it or we have jobs that seem meaningful and important, we are thereby endowed with a sense of being 'somebody.' When we experience the opposite, we fear that we are 'nobodies.' The nature of our occupations and the success we have in them are enormously powerful factors in our own sense of identity and well-being."

The longing that many of us have felt to be someone else or somewhere else or to be doing something else is almost unavoidable in a society that is so materially and externally driven. It's also understandable—for a time, anyway—as we seek to find our places in the great swarm of human activity and consciousness. Unfortunately, comparing our lives with someone else's and striving for things that we've been taught to want and using them as measures of our success ultimately leaves little room for what we could find out about ourselves and others if we examined things from a different perspective. Such a perspective may allow us to discover that in driving a cab or waiting tables, there are plenty of qualities that can elevate such work into a path of honor and self-expression: humility, mindfulness, patience, compassion, and so on. The challenge is to see all—or at least most—work as valuable and important and to disengage from society's fixation on equating success with power and wealth. Until we make peace with our places in the workaday world, there can be no satisfaction, economically or spiritually.

In re-viewing our work as something noble, as a place with all the spiritual potential of any monastery, we can create a space where such acceptance is within grasp. Martin Luther King Jr. once said, "If you are called to be a streetsweeper, you should sweep streets even as Michelangelo painted, or Beethoven composed music, or Shakespeare wrote poetry." Lord Tweedsmuir, author, statesman, and former Governor General of Canada, wrote, "I would be content with any job, however thankless, in any quarter, however remote, if I had a chance of making a corner of the desert blossom and a solitary place glad."

What beautiful expressions these are, and how well they capture the essence of what it means to be in service. What does it matter what work we do if we bring that kind of energy to it? Is this not our purpose on this planet? Guided by such a vision, we can begin to see our work as a grand opportunity to participate in life in a soulful and joyous way, no matter what it is that we do. The value lies in the doing of it and the spirit behind that doing, not in what others think. The satisfaction that follows when we give ourselves to work in this way resonates deep within, so deep that the boundaries between who we are and what we do begin to dissolve.

Organizational consultant Dick Richards calls this "artful"

work, which he describes as work that "requires the consistent and conscious use of the self. As the artist creates the work, the work creates the artist. . . . The materials of the moment are more than the physical things in front of us—more than simply the clay, a report from a task force, a page of numbers, a set of charts, a machine, or ideas written on a white board. The materials of the moment include emotion and spirit. When we include them, we become who we truly are and bring all of ourselves to our work. We become centered *and* artful."

Within this framework, such statements as "I wait tables," "I deliver mail," or "I _____," place the emphasis as much on the "I" as on whatever it is that follows. Importantly, this emphasis is even greater in service work, for it is in such work that self and other intersect, where meaningful contact can be made. Indeed, in a seemingly senseless, uncaring, and faceless world, we find meaning where we can, no less so a cab driver than a CEO—in a handshake, a smile, a simple act of kindness. This is what makes work so valuable, and service work especially so. For its role is crucial in the matrix of relationships that keeps the world from coming unglued. Knowing this can have a galvanizing impact on how we perceive the value of our work and its place in the story of our—as well as others'—lives.

Labor as an Act of God

There once lived a man who gathered wood
for a living. He had few customers and was
very poor, but never complained, and read the
Psalms daily. His wife was not happy and
implored him to find more lucrative work. He
answered, "The Lord is my shepherd, I shall
not want." One Passover, an old man knocked
at their door. "I would like to buy some fire-
wood," he said. After the wood gatherer sold a
large bundle to him, the customer (actually
the prophet Elijah in disguise) brushed against
a log of the house as he left; it turned to gold.
The couple now had enough money and the
man kept gathering wood and reading the
Psalms.

—ADAPTED FROM A JEWISH FOLKTALE

Boy now, I hope it's becoming clear that all work has value and that the work we do can play a vital role in the un-folding of our spiritual lives. Believing this makes it easier to take those first few steps toward embracing our jobs as partners on the spiritual path. This is important, because despite all the rhetoric directed at workplace transformation, most businesses play by old rules, and most jobs remain frozen in a fixed hierarchy of significance. Thus, once you commit to making work a spiritual path, you may feel as if you're the only one in your building, or on your beat, or wherever you ply your trade, who's "going off book," leaving the script and creating their own story.

By making your work an opportunity for spiritual growth, in which service is the ultimate expression, you'll join many others who feel the same call. It's a call that has echoed through the ages in the voice of many religious traditions, where work was honored as a vital ingredient of a rich spiritual life. The original theologies that emerged from the East and West have much in common in this regard. Each made it clear that a rich man was no closer to God than a poor one; that work was intrinsically a good thing, to be embraced with wholehearted commitment; and that work could—and should—be used as a means of devotional expression. John Cowan summarized this shared spiritual heritage in his book *The Common Table* when he wrote:

> *There is at least one scholar of the Christian scriptures who says that the reason Jesus of Nazareth angered the authorities enough to be crucified was that he ate at a common table. That was the sin for which he had to be punished, the cause of the accusations that he fomented trouble. He acted as if the rich were on the same level as the poor, the good wife the same level as the prostitute, the landowner and the heretic equally welcome to use similar utensils.*

> *As the legend goes, the Chinese philosopher Lao-tzu, leaving the city in disgust, was stopped by the gatekeeper and asked to leave his wisdom in writing so that the city would at least know what he was disgusted at. He wrote the* Tao Té Ching, *a poem to leaders insisting that they make themselves lower than their followers.*

The original Buddha found himself the bearer of the Buddha nature only after he set aside the trappings of the prince.

These powerful messages have become all but lost amidst the various cultural and economic realignments that have altered our beliefs about work since those wise teachers walked the Earth. The Reformation movement, the Industrial Revolution, and the Information Age and computer technology—each one has helped to reshape our notions of work and its place in Western society. The end result has been not only unprecedented wealth and convenience but also unprecedented anxiety and a planet that is buckling under the stress. To consider the role of spirituality in a twenty-first-century model of work, it will help to go back in time and observe how work was viewed in various religious and spiritual traditions.

Christianity and Work

There are many who will say that the West has made hard work and getting ahead into a religion, but a religion devoid of spiritual life. Some 2,000 years ago, Christ cautioned that it would be easier for a camel to pass through the eye of a needle than for a rich man to get to heaven. Not anymore, it seems. A popular news magazine, in discussing the remarkable financial achievements of the Mormon Church since its founding in the early 1800s, said that its hard-earned success was a reflection of our nation's moral declaration that "material achievement remains the earthly manifestation of virtue." Indeed, the Judeo-Christian work ethic has often been invoked as the driving force behind much of what is admirable about capitalism and the U.S. economy, not to mention its role—however unspoken—as a guarantor of religious salvation. How did this come to pass?

In the beginning (according to earliest Christian scripture), God probably said something like, "You will have work to do, lots of it, and it will be hard and boring because you deserve no better. But I have given you a mind and a pair of hands, and with them you will use work to honor me, to take care of the Earth that I have created, and to redeem yourselves as human beings made in my image. Or else . . ."

In pre-Reformation times, the material world was seen as something evil, something to escape. Poverty was extolled ("Blessed are you who are poor, for yours is the kingdom of God"—Luke 6:20), and the life of the mind was held in far more favorable regard than the life of commerce. Work was "a burden and a tribulation" that followed from original sin, "humankind's turning away from God and his plan."

At the same time, there were pockets of industriousness, albeit performed in service to the Almighty, that were precursors of today's unlikely marriage of virtue and affluence. One such pocket was found among the Benedictine monasteries of the sixth century; American philosopher and educator Lewis Mumford went so far as to suggest that the Benedictines were the founders of capitalism. Why? They considered work, along with prayer and recreation, as the primary means by which one could grow closer to God. In carrying out the various duties of their station, the inventive monks apparently found ways to standardize their tasks and create greater efficiencies, thus freeing themselves for more meditation and prayer time. When combined with their natural thriftiness, the result was a savings of money that was then reinvested in better tools, which saved even more time, and thus a pattern was set. They were literally working for God, from a place of total devotion and surrender.

English historian Arnold Toynbee drew comparisons between monasticism and capitalism when he considered that the monks' motivation was primarily *inner-directed*. "The

Benedictine Rule achieved what has never been achieved by the Gracchan agrarian laws of the Imperial alimenta," he writes, "because it worked, not as state action works, from above downwards, but from below upwards, by evoking the individual's initiative through enlisting his religious enthusiasm."

It was also a Benedictine, the abbess Hildegard of Bingen (whose popularity has soared in the past few years as a figure of mystic—and mythic—import), who in the twelfth century challenged the then-dominant notion of work as a toil to be endured when she said, "When humans do good work, they become a flowering orchard permeating the universe and making the cosmic wheel go around." In *The Reinvention of Work*, Matthew Fox interprets her declaration as having three implications: that when humans are working, they are flourishing; that "we are about good work"; and that when we aren't doing "good work," the cosmic wheel spins a little slower.

Meister Eckhart, another in the trio of influential medieval Christian mystics (the third was Thomas Aquinas) who sought to recast work in a more spiritual light, echoed Hildegard when he said that "through good works one puts forth the image of the heavenly person in themselves." And while the good works that he refers to include helping little old ladies across the street, they surely must encompass the other labors of our day. It wasn't until the Reformation of the 1500s, however, that work was finally transformed from a yoke of duty into a celebration of humanness in which perseverance, wealth, and salvation were equal partners.

The Reformation began as a movement within the Catholic Church to "revisit"—and in some cases, to challenge outright—certain assumptions about the nature of man's relationship with God and the Church. Preceding this insurrection and adding to the foment of the day were a number of fundamental changes in secular society, including the invention of the printing press, a growing middle class and merchant economy, and political conflicts between the Roman emperor and a restive Germany. Enter Martin Luther and John Calvin.

Luther was the German priest who, shocked by what he perceived as the spiritual laziness of papal Rome, came up with an alternate view of moral Christian living, hammered 95 theses on the door of a Saxon church, and started the Protestant religious movement. Calvin was a French Protestant theologian whose similar disputes with papal authority further altered the landscape of Christian spirituality. And while it was their pivotal role in the Reformation that historians are most apt to focus on, it was their views about work that sowed the seeds of the modern Judeo-Christian work ethic and its emphasis on frugality, industriousness, and moral rigor.

Luther brought a new perspective to the role of work in God's plan by introducing the idea of work as *vocation*, a calling in which an individual uses all of his skills and intentions to serve God by serving others. "For Luther," writes James M. Childs Jr. in *Ethics in Business: Faith at Work*, "vocation is realized through the various 'stations' we occupy in life: parenting, citizenship, marriage, work, profession, and so on. These are roles and relationships that God has established to benefit all people, and all who participate in them participate in that plan. For Christians in particular, the stations of life are conduits for the loving service of people . . ."

These observations are echoed by Oliver Williams and John Houck, who wrote in their book *The Judeo-Christian Vision and the Modern Corporation*: "Luther taught that one's occupation in the world was not to be taken lightly, for doing the task well was the way to serve God and to give thanks for divine justification. This conviction provided motivation for high performance in one's station in life, whether it be as a scholar, craftsperson, or laborer."

Calvin's contribution was to conclude that since everything came from God, work had its place at the Lord's table, especially as it made life better for all: "We know that men were created for the express purpose of being employed in labor of various kinds and that no sacrifice is more pleasing to God than when every man applies diligently to his own calling and endeavors to live in such a manner as to contribute to the general advantage." For Calvin, one worked for the glory of God; by serving others, one served God.

There were a couple of catches in Calvin's vision, though. The most troublesome was his doctrine of predestination. It essentially declared that a person's destiny at the end of life was already preordained by God, and there was little that anyone could do to alter it: You were either chosen or you weren't. This, of course, led to a great deal of "salvation anxiety," as many people agonized over their fate. How is one to know? Is it a matter of faith, birth, roulette?

It was left to the newly Reformed pastors to step forward and offer some guidance. They said that there were signs by which a person could know his fate, and one of those was material success. Prosperity was one indication that you would be saved. People worked diligently to ensure that their businesses were profitable, but because they were encouraged by the clergy to be frugal, they also strove for a humble and austere lifestyle. This combination is what we now refer to as the Protestant work ethic.

Unfortunately, Calvin also preached that wealth was a scourge if it caused people to value it above holiness and commitment to God in their work. To this the pastors had another answer: the doctrine of stewardship, which held that wealth was a trust to be kept for the common good. This final flourish brought full circle the notions raised hundreds of years earlier by Matthew in the New Testament when he wrote the parable of the talents.

The story concerned a feudal master and his three stewards. The master, about to leave on a long journey, asked each of his charges to watch over sums of money that he would leave with them during his absence. Two of the stewards invested wisely and doubled their master's money; the third steward buried his in the ground. Upon the master's return, the first two stewards were rewarded for their initiative and invited to "enter into the joy of (their) master"; the third, "the wicked and slothful servant," was cast out of the house.

This story has been interpreted as having several meanings or moral lessons, among them the belief that work is a gift, a calling and a blessing from God. It follows that since work is really vocation, it demands a wholehearted and enthusiastic commitment to service, stewardship, and moral responsibility. And finally, it's God, not society, who will decide the value of our effort. Therefore, the rewards of good work may not be necessarily financial. In the parable above, financial rewards do not even enter the picture. Instead, it's the dedication and service shown by the workers that will get them into Heaven. This ultimate confluence of vocation, stewardship, hard work, frugality, and God ushered in what German sociologist Max Weber called the "fundamental element of the spirit of modern capitalism: rational conduct on the basis of calling."

There are some, however, who feel that while the Protestant work ethic is still the defining characteristic of work in the West, it has lost its religious underpinnings and even, perhaps, its soul, by condoning great wealth and high moral ground at the expense of the greater good. Conservative writer Sir Fred Catherwood expressed his concern in 1983 that the original spirit of the Protestant work ethic was "in visible decline. . . . The Christian doctrine of work should lead to the creation of wealth, not by the destruction of the world's natural resources but by their proper use. Christians believe that mankind holds the natural resources of the world in trust from God and that these should not only be passed on to succeeding generations intact but, as in the parable of the talents . . . improved in the passing."

Childs compares the ideals of Christian business ethics with the realities of today's workplace and says in effect that the vast inequities in the current system regarding salaries and status are hardly evidence that "the biblical ideal is at work." Further, he summarizes the work of others writing in the field by stating that "commitment to a 'religion' of conspicuous achievement as the key to meaning in life can be a harsh and demanding regimen that could cause us to compromise our own best qualities and some of our most precious values."

The message seems to be that we in the West have broken free from the moorings of a truly moral work life and that it is time to reconsider our successes and the price we have paid to achieve them. The door thus opens to a new view of work that restores the integrity of the original Christian vision: work as a calling and a stewardship that puts the spirit of God back into the bottom line.

Eastern Economics and Skillful Means

In Buddhism, a dominant religion of the East with a growing following in the West, the Noble Eightfold Path of the Middle Way represents the means by which an individual can free himself from suffering, make contact with his truest nature, and live a fuller, richer life. Each of the eight "folds" in this path, as put forth by the Buddha 2,500 years ago, deals with some aspect of wisdom, morality, and self-awareness/inner journeying.

The first of these folds, called Right Views, urges a perspective that sees all life as interdependent and part of the same creation, yet one that is unflinching in its desire to know the truth of "what is" without bias or distortion. Right Thought has to do with the motives and the vision behind our actions and the power of the mind to enable transformation. Right Speech is about paying attention to our words: Do we speak truth, kindness, and clarity, or gossip, deceit, and lies?

Right Action is about what we actually do in the world: Do we "walk our talk" or diminish ourselves and our world by thoughtless activities?

In Right Effort, the emphasis is on using the will to awaken ourselves to higher consciousness and overcome the various influences that can knock us off the path. Right Mindfulness and Right Contemplation, living in the now in total balance, provide the final tools for achieving a state of mind in which, as author and educator Claude Whitmyer writes, "our intellectual understanding of the Eightfold Path evolves into an experiential one. Having overcome the obstacles to the comprehension of life as it really is, we manifest spontaneous, unmotivated action completely appropriate to the present moment."

The one fold that I have not yet mentioned is Right Livelihood, which essentially urges work that does no harm, in which practitioners use their work to show their love of the world. Zen practitioner Les Kaye defines Right Livelihood more austerely as the practice of work that helps one "to utilize and develop [his or her] abilities, to experience the dropping away of ego when joining with others in common tasks, and to build character" while providing for the needs of the community. Such perspectives are quite unlike those of the modern West, where work is more often than not considered a necessary evil that we must endure while pursuing other treasures. In Buddhism, Kaye writes, "work and leisure are merely two sides of the same coin, and . . . the coin itself is the total expression of spiritual life."

E. F. Schumacher was a well-known British economist who extolled the virtues of appropriate scale, craftsmanship, and community as he argued against the dominance of the capitalistic paradigm. He saw the Buddhist approach to work as offering a much more humane alternative to the economic system of the West, where working folks are dehumanized as "units of production," full employment is considered economically undesirable, and the Gross National Product is worshiped like a god. "To organize work in such a manner that it becomes meaningless, boring, stultifying, or nerve-wracking for the worker would be little short of criminal," he writes. "From a Buddhist point of view, this is standing the truth on its head by considering goods as more important than people and consumption as more important than creative activity . . . the Buddhist sees the essence of civilization not in a multiplication of wants but in the purification of human character. Character, at the same time, is formed primarily by a man's work. And work, if properly conducted in conditions of human dignity and freedom, blesses those who do it and equally their products."

Since Buddhism's main concern is liberation from desire, not the goods that we accumulate, it would seem that its true path follows closely the edges of basic human survival, for as the Buddha once said, "Let us live most happily, possessing nothing; let us feed on joy, like radiant gods." But as Schumacher explains, the Middle Way of Buddhism is not averse to physical comfort. "It is not wealth that stands in the way of liberation but the attachment to wealth; not the enjoyment of pleasurable things but the craving for them. The keynote of Buddhist economics, therefore, is simplicity and nonviolence. From an economist's point of view, the marvel of the Buddhist way of life is the utter rationality of its pattern—amazingly small means leading to extraordinarily satisfactory results."

The Buddha realized that the work we do must be consonant with all of the other precepts of the Middle Way, which to him meant laboring in occupations that do not harm other creatures or destroy the environment. He was specifically against such things as prostitution and the merchant trade as it pertained to the sale of slaves, arms, poisons, and the like. He was against alcohol and the killing of animals. Living today, however, and facing the complexities of a modern world where such things have become commonplace, he might simply shake his head and abandon society to fend for itself. Or, as historian and scholar Huston Smith reflects, he might moderate his views, but only somewhat. "While the Buddha's explicit teachings about work were aimed at helping his contemporaries decide between occupations that were conducive to spiritual progress and ones that impeded it, there are Buddhists who suggest that if he were teaching today, he would be less concerned with specifics than with the danger that people forget that earning a living is life's means, not life's ends."

Tarthang Tulku, a religious teacher from the Tarthang Monastery in eastern Tibet and author of several books on the subject of Right Livelihood, says about work: "Caring about our work, liking it, even loving it, seems strange when we see work only as a way to make a living. But when we see work as the way to deepen and enrich all our experiences, each one of us can find this caring within our hearts and waken it in those around us, using every aspect of work to learn and grow."

A similar approach is found in Hinduism in the practice of *karma yoga*, or "the path of God through work." Such a path arose out of the acknowledgment that one's work life needn't be separate from one's spiritual life, that God can be found anywhere, at any time. To limit that experience to certain times of the day or week is to limit the opportunities for sacred expression.

Practitioners of karma yoga seek to dissolve the ego and material desires from the work they do in the world, replacing them with a selfless devotion to manifesting the spirit of God in all of their actions. They become, in essence, instruments for God's energy, in effect channeling higher intentions. "Performed in this spirit," Smith writes, "action lightens the ego instead of encumbering it. Each task becomes a sacred ritual, lovingly fulfilled as a living sacrifice to God's glory. . . . Surrendering to the Lord of all, [the practitioner] remains untouched by life's vicissitudes. Such people are not broken by discouragements, for winning is not what motivates them; they want only to be on the right side." In this way, work becomes one's *sadhana*, or "effective means of attainment," the path that leads to spiritual wisdom.

In the sacred Hindu text *Bhagavad Gita*, a philosophical dialogue between Lord Krishna and Prince Arjuna on the eve of a great battle, much is written about work as a form of spiritual expression:

> *Know therefore what is work, and also what is wrong work. . . . One whose undertakings are free from anxious desire and fanciful thought, whose work is made pure in the fire of wisdom: that one is called wise by those who see. In whatever work she does such a person in truth has peace: she expects nothing, relies on nothing, and ever has fullness of joy . . . He is glad with whatever God gives him . . . he is without jealousy, and in success or in failure is one: his works bind him not. He has attained liberation, is free from all bonds, his mind has found peace in wisdom, and his work is a holy sacrifice. The work of such a person is pure.*

Mahatma Gandhi, whose nonviolence campaign against the ruling British in his home country of India changed history, was a devoted disciple of the *Bhavagad Gita*. He first studied it in his twenties while going to law school in England, then embraced it further when he moved to South Africa, where it became his "spiritual reference book." It was in South Africa that he had his first experience of work in which the goal of winning took a distant second to serving a higher good.

He had been struggling with a string of failures, personal as well as professional, and the death of his beloved mother.

Not only that, his arrival on this distant continent brought him face-to-face with racial discrimination, an indignity he had never known. His first case involved disagreements about money between two parties who were blood relatives. He thought that trying the case would require knowledge that he didn't possess. He also knew that he could turn it down and finish his 12-month commitment to the law firm simply by attending to "minor correspondence," and then returning to India when he was finished. Instead, he threw himself completely into the matter.

He learned everything about it that he could and realized that the facts were on his client's side. He also concluded, however, that if the case went to trial, a long court battle would be unavoidable, driving family members farther apart. So he took another tack: talking to both sides and convincing them to settle out of court. As Eknath Easwaran writes in his biography of Gandhi:

> *Gandhi was ecstatic. "I had learned," [Gandhi] exclaimed, "the true practice of law. I had learnt to find out the better side of human nature and to enter men's hearts. I realized that the true function of a lawyer was to unite parties riven asunder." Without realizing it, Gandhi had found the secret of success. He began to look on every difficulty as an opportunity for service, a challenge which could draw out of him greater resources of intelligence and imagination. In turning his back on personal profit or prestige in his work, he found he had won the trust and even love of white and Indian South Africans alike.*

The idea of work as a means of spiritual devotion had an influential champion in the person of Suzuki Shōsan, a Zen practitioner who lived in the 1600s. In fact, one writer considers him "the father of Japanese capitalism," although an inadvertent one, to be sure. This particular period in Japan's history was one of relative peace and stability following a time of civil unrest and samurai warfare. In an article entitled, "Zen and the Economic Animal," Yamamoto Shichihei writes that despite such a relief from bloodshed, people "lost sight of their reason for living." Enter Shōsan, who "sought to resolve their distress by finding a spiritual meaning in everyday labor" through the application of Buddhist principles. This was aimed at the working classes of the time, who worried that because they weren't priests, blessedly engaged in devotional activity, it would be impossible for them to achieve their Buddha nature and manifest an enlightened society.

Shōsan's prescription was to urge citizens to see labor as an aspect of Buddhist practice that should be engaged in wholeheartedly, thus freeing them from the "three poisons" of greed, anger, and discontent.

> *The all-encompassing Buddha-nature manifest in us all works for the world's good: without artisans, such as the blacksmith, there would be no tools; without officials there would be no order in the world; without farmers there would be no food; without merchants we would suffer inconvenience. All the other occupations as well are for the good of the world . . . All reveal the blessing of the Buddha.*

And so labor, and even profit, were good things, even sacred things, if they flowed out of good intentions and a totally honest relationship with others. For a merchant to achieve a Buddha nature, he would have to travel around distributing his goods as if it were a pilgrimage. Such a view is not unlike that of the Christian who, in pursuing his vocation with moral integrity and stewarding his resources wisely, pleases God and shows that he is worthy of heavenly admission.

In this twentieth century of self-exploration and discovery, there is a converging of means and ends as they relate to our work life and growing recognition that they can be found wherever we set our feet. Right Livelihood has as much to do with how we do what we do as with what we do, and service work is the ideal place to discover this. Indeed, we can turn any job into Right Livelihood by using it as a place to truly serve others, a practice that ultimately serves ourselves. In Sanskrit, the word *upaya* stands for "skillful means" or "the craft of compassion," a compassion that flows from the idea of Right Views, the belief that all life is sacred. When we serve others with compassion and honesty, when our intent is to give, when the outcome of our actions is to lighten another's load, we are doing our spiritual work.

I heard a story not too long ago about a fellow who worked as an attendant in an underground parking garage. It seems that the guy who used to have the job treated it as we might expect with the kind of work where the people you serve are probably no more conscious of you than they would be of an automated teller machine. And who among us could really blame him? Dark, repetitive, isolated, subterranean—it's an atmosphere that's more likely to twist a psyche than to nurture one.

So then this new person came in, and suddenly things started to feel different. He cleaned up the entrance, placed signs to help visitors find the elevators, and warmly greeted everyone he met. Said one office employee: "I never realized how poor a job the other person was doing. Frank gives me a little boost in the morning that was never there before." He took his work seriously and made it his own. He showed pride in what he did, acted with good intention, and exhibited mindfulness and compassion. In so doing, he had the potential of affecting each of the 500 people who worked in that office building every day that he was there. This is Right

Livelihood by any spiritual measure, for in the simple tasks of his job were found the means to be a shining light.

The Native American Voice

The storytelling traditions of North America's indigenous tribes speak a great deal about the value that they placed on community, appropriate livelihood, and honoring the Spirit within all things. They also reflect the people's intimate relationships with the land on which they lived, which was the provider of their food and shelter and the teacher of the ways of their ancestors.

The tales that follow, handed down for generations and known to many modern storytellers, all address some aspect of daily work, including its importance to a tribe's communal health and as a tool for an individual's growth. Each of them contains the message that it matters not what the work is, only that it's done well and in the right spirit.

A Southwest tribal tale, for example, tells of a boy who desired to fly with the eagles instead of hoeing the corn, squash, and beans with the other members of his tribe. His unwillingness to embrace the ways of his people upset many in the community, who resolved to kill the eagle that had become the boy's pet. The boy and his eagle escaped, barely, and then fled to the Kingdom of the Eagles atop Turquoise Mountain. There, the boy's time was filled with the delights of soaring, and he couldn't have been happier. His eagle brothers warned him of only one thing: Whatever you do, they cautioned, you shouldn't fly south.

Well, you can't tell a young boy what *not* to do, and eventually curiosity got the best of him. He flew south, where he discovered a world of utter self-indulgence that seemed at first to be the answer to his dreams. He decided to stay, of course, but the life he chose—luxury and wanton feasting by night, a zombie-like existence by day—drained his life force, finally robbing him of his eagle power. Terrified and feeling powerless, chased by the walking dead, he ended up falling into a badger hole.

Grandfather Badger decided to take the boy in, and he taught him a different way of living in which the needs of others were as important (and sometimes more so) as his own. Many lessons and many trials later, the young man realized the Grandfather's truths, returned to his village, and took up his hoe gratefully. From that day on, once every year, his tribe had a day of Eagle Dances, and the boy told his story. The young ones sat wide-eyed and solemn, the elders nodded knowingly, and then the boy returned to the field and tilled the soil without complaint.

                                                                                  ●

The Zunis tell of a young girl who was given the job of herding the turkeys that were raised in her village. It was far from glamorous work: It was dusty and boring, working alone in the vast desert while others made ceremonial objects or went off on big hunts. Sure enough, the girl lost interest and filled her time with daydreams of a different life. The turkeys disappeared into the canyon. Realizing her mistake, she frantically tried to find them, but to no avail—they were gone. When she returned to the village without them, the people were furious.

"How could you do this?" they cried. "You were supposed to watch them. Those turkeys are very important to us."

They sent the girl away, saying that she couldn't come back until she found the turkeys. She left, crestfallen. In some versions of the tale, the girl never returned, and she wandered forever in the canyons, haunted, calling for her turkeys.

The image of the eagle, a frequent symbol of spiritual power, plays a prominent role in a Tlingit tale. A young boy, weak of limb, liked to go to the river alone and catch fish, then feed them to the eagles, praying that he would gain some of their vision and power. The chief of the village wondered what the boy did with all of his time, saying that he should be fishing with the others because they provided for the needs of the village. The boy resisted, knowing that the others fished in large canoes and bragged about their prowess and great catches. He was not so robust, and anyway, he just didn't fit in.

Old Aunty loved the boy and gave him herbs to strengthen him physically as well as spiritually. When the chief finally discovered what the boy and his aunt were up to, he was furious. How dare they disobey him! He decided to leave them behind when the rest of the villagers departed for their winter camp. The boy and his aunt were devastated. "Whatever will we do?" they worried.

It was a brutal and difficult winter, and the boy and his aunt nearly starved—until an eagle brought them a fish. Gratefully, they ate the food and wondered at the unexpected gift. But the blessings didn't end. The eagles kept bringing them food, sometimes a rabbit, sometimes more fish, sometimes as much as an entire whale. The two devised ways to harvest the food, working hard to skin, butcher, and store it. When the tribe returned in the spring, starving and without resources, the Eagle Boy happily provided food for all. He had gained special vision and insight, which the villagers then realized. Not long thereafter, he became chief of his tribe, and his people lived a good and abundant life.

To this day, the Tlingit believe that some of their catch must be left for the eagles, and at least one of the great canoes must be decorated with the eagle emblem.

Here, the young boy is on a quest from the very beginning, rejecting those who seem more intent on bigger and better and choosing instead to humbly serve the calling of his heart. His persistence and faith pay off—although not without trial and challenge—and he is rewarded by Great Spirit for his efforts. Had he chosen differently, joining the others in their endless pursuit of the largest fish, he would never have discovered his true gifts. The loss would not have been just his own; the entire village would have suffered.

A very dear friend of mine who guides people in understanding Native American ways notes that in depicting cross-species communication and relationships in this way, this story goes into that mystical experience where we know at a deep level that all is one; that all things are alive, have a spirit, and are sentient; and that everything is interdependent. "This is not just a philosophical thought," she says, "but an actual happening, as when the eagle gives food to another life form so that it may live. The actions of the generations that follow this event show that they honor the gift of Spirit and the gift of the spirit of the eagle. Being of service cannot truly happen until one realizes how dependent we all are."

This idea of essential interconnectedness is also embodied in Navajo principles. According to businessman/medicine man Robert Preston, this is the Navajo tradition of honoring what he calls the beauty of the ancients and the natural wisdom of the universe. It's the principle of seeing everyone, not just the elders or the experts but also "the man laying bricks, the person planting flowers," as potential teachers. To acknowledge in the grocery store clerk the same spark of value and innate knowledge as we might assume for a doctor or a visiting diplomat is to widen our respect for those who walk this earth with us, no matter their circumstance. Someone who follows such a path does so with a "spiritual mind," one in which the head and the heart are married in a belief that all of life is sacred. It's about walking our talk, feeling the rightness of what we're doing, being connected to it from the inside, and wanting to give back to our community out of a spirit of generosity and a genuine feeling of kinship.

The "give-away" has a long history in Native American tradition. It has to do with giving back to the world what you have received from it as you "go around the wheel of life," accumulating the experiences that are shaping you as a human being. Among indigenous peoples in the past, such gifts included buckskins, jewelry, baskets, and ceremonial objects. Today, they might be blankets, food, tools, or clothing. What is given doesn't matter as long as it's done without expectation of return. When we engage in our own version of the give-away—sharing our knowledge, our love, the gift of who we are—we serve others in the spirit in which such service has greatest impact.

Carried into the workplace, this idea can have a transformative impact on everything we do and everyone whose path we cross. By continually asking ourselves how work can help us give back to the world around us, we bring a spiritual dimension to our jobs that can be expressed in the simplest of gestures, making certain moments special that would otherwise get lost in the jungle of our daily demands.

Means over Ends

We have tended to forget that at the core of many major spiritual traditions lies a firm belief in the importance and goodness of everyday labor. Terms such as *vocation, stewardship, Right Livelihood*, and *service* were an acceptable part of the work ethic. More often than not, work was the means to a material as well as a spiritual end, a form of devotion fully integrated into spiritual and religious practices.

Today, those noble intentions have shown the wear of competing—unsuccessfully—with an almost insatiable preoccupation with material success and ego gratification. What we've created is a picture of work in which the ends are favored over the means, certain kinds of jobs are held in higher esteem than others, and drudgery is a defining characteristic. While there are signs of change—visionary corporate leaders and risk-taking individuals who are seeking work on their own terms—the changes are slow to come, and in some places, they may never arrive. Most of the work being done is the product of generations of beliefs about what work is—and isn't. For most of us, work is a road, not a destination, a road that's badly in need of repair. But we don't really expect anyone to come around and fix it, and there doesn't seem to be much that one person can do, so we just go along, day in and day out, uncomfortably sandwiched between hope and despair.

Given such a system of beliefs, it's no wonder that work has been devalued, stripped of much of what it could be. The monetary rewards clothe and feed us and keep us out of the cold, but seldom does work itself nurture our spirits. This is a shame, because it takes up so much of our time.

The work that we do can, and ultimately must, be an activity in which we exercise our will toward transformation despite what may seem like a conspiracy of dispiriting circumstances. Look first to yourself; draw inspiration from the examples presented above. In using work as a spiritual path, anyone can be a leader, a role model, a trendsetter, a paradigm buster. Parking lot attendants, housewives, bank tellers, waiters—all can be found on the cutting edge of what it means to be living and working a meaningful life. All it takes is a commitment to change and a realization that in the myriad moments of your working day lie an abundance of tools and opportunities for birthing your spiritual self.

The Tao of Tea

Small service is true service. . . . The daisy,
by the shadow that it casts, protects the
lingering dewdrop from the sun.
—WILLIAM WORDSWORTH

Chado, or The Way of Tea, is a time-honored tradition in Japanese culture, expressed in the deceptively simple act of serving tea. The reason it has been called a "way" derives from the nearly lifelong process of self-discipline and learning that's required to master its finest art, a lineage of training and knowledge that is centuries old.

There is a popular story about the tea ceremony (or *chanoyu,* which literally means "hot water for tea") that beautifully illustrates the essence of this ancient practice. It comes from the sixteenth century and concerns Sen Rikyu, who is considered by many historians to be the most influential among Japan's few truly great tea masters. It seems that a student once asked Rikyu about the secret of tea. "Suggest coolness in the summer and warmth in winter," he replied. "Set the charcoal so that water will boil. The flowers should be arranged as if they were still in the field."

"Anyone can do that," the student responded.

"If that is so," said Rikyu, "then I will become your student and you will be my teacher."

For its practitioners, *Chado* is an ultimate way of life, a consummate philosophy of being and doing that, in its simplicity and depth, contains all the tools for living a spiritual life. What I find most compelling about the tea ceremony—which essentially includes the choice of utensils, the cleaning and decoration of the room, various stages of psychological and spiritual preparation, and the actual serving of the tea—is this focus on *doing* as the principal means of expression, a doing that not only seeks to experience the ultimate beauty in things but that also represents an active form of spiritual discipline. Such intention has important lessons for anyone who is striving to transform their work into something sacred.

My first introduction to the tea ceremony was at a busy conference in the Midwest. My days—and nights—were filled with appointments and seminars and working in my company's booth; slipping out for a moment of peace was a challenge that even Houdini would have found daunting. It happened that one of the vendors at the show was representing a Japanese publisher, and one of the books that they were featuring was about the tea ceremony. I didn't know much about it, only what I had gleaned from reading or movies, but the thought of just sitting down and having a nice cup of tea was overwhelmingly seductive.

Despite the similarity of the venue—a hotel meeting room—to the world I had just escaped, what I found occurring inside was decidedly unconventional. The mood was serene despite the more than 40 milling people and a buffet of catered niblets. Several kimono-clad hosts and a few well-placed artistic flourishes—a sculpted Buddha and Oriental vases of impeccably arranged flowers—offered a refreshing distraction from the Styrofoam and sameness of the show.

After a few minutes of getting our bearings, we were all

asked to sit down. A robed, middle-aged Japanese man then stepped from behind a parchment partition, which featured long-legged storks and drooping high grasses, and greeted us with a bow. We all grew silent, and although what followed was not an actual tea ceremony but a shortened and more informal version, it was just the tonic I needed, inspiring me to learn more about this 500-year-old tradition.

A Short History

I was surprised to learn that tea had a long and magical history, steeped in meaning. *Matcha*, or powdered green tea, first arrived in Japan in the twelfth century, brought back from China by monks returning from their studies at China's great Zen monasteries. At that time, its use was primarily medicinal, but it was also an adjunct to Zen study and meditation (the monks, it seems, would drink great amounts of it to remain awake during their extended meditation practices). A few centuries later, tea became something of a party beverage and a respite from the warfare of the time, the focus of lavish ceremonies and tea-tasting contests hosted by ruling shoguns.

At the turn of the fifteenth century, a new spirit emerged around tea, influenced greatly by the Zen priest Murata Shuko, who felt that *chanoyu* should become much more of a spiritual art. Shuko brought a more refined and thoughtful energy to the practice, replacing the great tea halls with smaller rooms and showy serving implements with simpler, domestic utensils. In *The World in a Bowl of Tea*, Bettina Vitell writes that Shuko "valued human relationships and emotions more than sensuous objects; he was the first to display calligraphy of a Zen master with words that appealed to the spirit of a person." Shuko's contribution was to show that tea was much more than just entertainment or even good medicine; it could be an expression of the Zen belief that every act has the potential of bringing us closer to enlightenment, to an experience of ultimate truth.

Takeno Jo-o further refined Shuko's minimalist style by introducing the idea of *wabi*, or the art of imperfection, into the art of tea ceremony. "[Jo-o] reinvented the *chanoyu* art form," writes Vitell. "He defined crude, 'low-tech' Japanese ceramics as *wabi*, a plain and unpolished beauty found in irregular and unfinished qualities of an object. He paired a rough, dull brown Bizen water jar with a pristine Chinese tea bowl. He arranged freshly gathered flowers in a cracked and misshapen Shigaraki vase."

The idea of *wabi* has poignant relevance to the issues raised in this book in that it is all about ennobling the ordinary and finding the beauty in the everyday. These tea masters were interested not in rare Chinese serving bowls or water kettles but in what might be found in any local farmer's kitchen.

Soetsu Yanagi, a student of Japanese arts, writes, "Most of us today have grown so commonplace that we cannot see the extraordinary save in the exceptional. The early Tea Masters apprehended the profundity of normal things. . . . [They] found a profounder beauty in the practical art born to answer the immediate needs of life than in the fine arts born to beauty's sake alone. They did not seek beauty apart from actual living. They found the highest and noblest aspects of beauty in the articles close to life."

And so it can be with our work, where "the articles close to life" represent all of the tools and tasks engaged in the cleaning, fixing, and serving that make up the majority of our active world. From washing a spoon to filing a nail to answering a phone to tightening a bolt, the message is clear: Look no farther than what is in front of you to find the keys to a more spiritual life.

Sen Rikyu, Jo-o's student, made *wabi* the centerpiece of *chanoyu*, and his contributions to the aesthetics of the tea ceremony are legendary; in fact, he had a lasting influence on many aspects of Japanese art and culture. However, it is his articulation of the Zen-like principles behind *Chado* that's particularly interesting, especially as they relate to our own approaches to work.

The true spirit of *Chado*, stated Rikyu, encompasses four characteristics—harmony (*wa*), respect (*kei*), purity (*sei*), and tranquillity (*jaku*)—which represent not just the practical nature of tea but also its highest ideals. These four qualities must be present for a tea ceremony to be considered successful. They also inform the day-to-day thoughts and activities of those who are students of *Chado*. The Way of Tea, it is said, cannot really be taught anyway; it is a state of mind, a "living" tradition, and the tea ceremony is only the most visible expression of that path.

Harmony, the first of these principles, implies a fluidity and balance of movement and energy: between the tea master, his utensils, and his guests; among the guests themselves; and in what the tea master uses to prepare and serve the tea—the bowls, the water container and ladle, the incense, the flower vase, and so on. As without, so within, and the harmony that is sought between and among things and people must also be present inside one's heart and mind. "The principle of harmony," writes Soshitsu Sen XV, grand master of the Urasenke School of Tea and author of *Tea Life, Tea Mind*, "means to be free of pretensions, walking the path of moderation, becoming neither heated or cold, and never forgetting the attitude of humility."

In a formal tea ceremony, *kei*, or respect, provides structure and etiquette, informing participants on what to wear, how to enter a room, where to sit, how to bow, and how to hold the cup and drink the tea. Beyond the ceremony, however, when we are *living* tea, *kei* "is the sincerity of heart that liberates us for an open relationship . . . [pressing] us to look deeply into the hearts of all people we meet and at the things in our environment. It is then that we realize our kinship with all the world around us," explains Soshitsu Sen XV. *Kei*, then, also implies acceptance in its deepest sense, for when we truly accept others, regardless of their station in life or what they are presenting us in the moment, we give ourselves permission to honor them as human beings, and in so doing, we honor ourselves.

The third principle, purity, refers to cleanliness and order, to which the tea master pays tribute as he prepares the tea room and the utensils, serves the tea, gathers and stores the utensils, and finally, closes the tea room. Ideally, the sacred space that the tea master creates in the tea room is internalized as he carries out his various tasks. This not only serves his own spiritual needs but also allows him to properly serve his guests, for it is only after such clearing has taken place that the sacred essence of man and nature becomes clear, and he can thus engage the outside world from a place of wisdom and compassion. The sanctuary of a properly "energized" tea room provides the opportunity to be touched by such an experience, not just for the tea master but for the guests as well, who have also been clearing from their hearts and minds the debris of the day, the cares and anxieties, the various attachments and considerations that keep the modern human brain occupied.

Tranquillity is the outcome when the first three principles are diligently practiced. It is something of an active meditation, an "in the world but not of the world" state of mind that the architects of *Chado* had always hoped to achieve. Isolated study and training is not required, and, in fact, can be counterproductive. Soshitsu Sen XV writes that, "tranquillity will deepen even further when another person enters the microcosm of the tea room and joins the host in contemplation over a bowl of tea. That we can find lasting tranquillity within our own selves in the company of others is the paradox."

This observation is especially important as we contemplate our places of work, seeing them not as distractions from the path but as part of the path itself. By striving to perform our jobs in a conscious fashion, we can learn and apply valuable spiritual lessons and in so doing, affect the people around us in a way that pleasantly lingers, as an experience of beauty stays with us even after the actual moment has passed. Some comments from modern-day students of *Chado* reveal the powerful impact that *chanoyu* has on practitioners. Their observations suggest that what is learned about the serving of tea is relevant well beyond the ceremony itself.

> *Directing the heart and mind toward providing for another person leaves no room for vanity or greed. The complete and sincere consideration for other people and nature which is displayed in the Way of Tea is an expression of true human morality.*

> *When one serves tea, that is all that one does. In order to serve tea properly, one must have the proper mind. If one's mind is not directed, it will wander to other things. The tea will be too hot or too cold, too strong or too weak. Steps will be eliminated. . . . All activities are like this. How can one drive safely during rush hour if one's mind is lost in thought? . . . Everything we do should be a single-minded effort, directed toward the task at hand. So, while we may not drink tea every day, tea is part of our everyday lives.*

Taking Time

Thus, it's the day-in and day-out manifesting of this spirit that makes *Chado* a way of life and a good model from which to draw inspiration, not just to guide us in our work but also to remind us that work is—or at least should be—a natural part of our spiritual path. The challenges we find in it are no different from those that we might experience anywhere else. The highly formalized nature of *Chado* and *chanoyu* does makes it seem, at least on the surface, an unreasonable comparison to the controlled frenzy of someplace like a downtown Burger King, but the principles behind them and some of the qualities associated with those principles—patience, skill, sincerity, focus, humility, precision, and so on—can apply to any kind of work. Kandis Susol, who has been a practitioner of the tea ceremony for 13 years, also owns her own beauty salon. She sees many parallels between the spirit that is invoked in *chanoyu* and what can be created in our daily work.

> *For me, bringing tea into everyday life began several years after my initial training. With all of the preparation before a ceremony, I started to understand how it's all connected to the moment in time that will never be the same. This realization slowly crept into other areas of my life, but mostly into my work as a hairdresser. Having the salon clean and ready to offer any service to a client all relates back to appropriateness and setting, and to acknowledging the way that everything is part of the same thing. When doing a tea ceremony, my consciousness is connected to the tea, the bowl, the spirit of my heart, and everyone and everything in the tea room. It's the same when I cut hair; the implements may be different, but the spirit is not.*

At the same time, as we might expect from a tradition as "formless" as Zen—one that has never been comfortable with Western attempts to define it—there is paradox in its emphasis on doing and de-emphasis of results. Rand Castille, a Westerner who for many years has studied the tea ceremony, writes in *The Way of Tea* that it's easy to make more of *chanoyu* than it is: the simple serving of tea and sharing some time with friends. He cautions those in the West not to elevate it to some kind of antidote for our spiritual ills; there is no "sudden enlightenment," he says. What happens simply makes life "more." He credits the thirteenth-century Zen master Dogen with capturing the essence of this non-process:

> *Our attainment of enlightenment is something like the reflection of the moon in water. The moon does not get wet, nor is the water cleft apart. Though the light of the moon is vast and immense, it finds a home in water only a foot long and an inch wide. The whole moon and the whole sky find room enough in a single dewdrop, a single drop of water. And just as the moon does not cleave the water apart, so enlightenment does not tear man apart. Just as a dewdrop or drop of water offers no resistance to the moon in heaven, so man offers no obstacle to the full penetration of enlightenment.*

6

Preparations
of the Spirit

I remember standing at a table as a couple
was getting ready to order. I was looking
at the woman in what I can only describe
as an instant of recognition. We were
talking about food, but I felt that we were
sharing an unspoken understanding of our
common humanness. In that moment, I
experienced this veil lift, this thing that
I carried between me and other people. I
never expected to feel this way at work,
to experience someone really seeing me.
I thought, "Wow! I can learn to be real
with people here."

—MARGARET, A WAITRESS

It took seven years for Margaret to reach this "A-ha"
point at her job, when she realized that work could be so
much more than just a paycheck. Margaret, who outside of
her workplace had an active spiritual life, hadn't really thought
much about the potential of her waitressing job as an oppor-

tunity for spiritual practice, or even as a place where she could simply be herself.

Margaret's moment of recognition was the awareness that meaningful experiences are not confined to church or a meditation pillow or next month's weekend retreat. Just because she was working, she realized, life's magic didn't stop. When she connected with that woman in what could be described as a soul-to-soul exchange, a light went on (in the wonderful and unexpected way that those things happen), and her whole experience of work shifted. More specifically, her whole experience of waitressing shifted.

Perhaps because Margaret did have a spiritual context in the rest of her life, her moment was waiting to happen. Whether or not this is true for the rest of us is less important, however, than the fact that we have made work less than it could be because we've never been trained to think otherwise. Work, we have come to believe, has only a limited capacity to feed our deeper needs. As a result, many of us have turned off certain parts of our humanity—the intuitive, the compassionate, the *conscious* parts—because we aren't able to see any place for them in the sometimes-mercenary gestalt of our workplaces.

To turn this state of affairs around, to consider work as an ally on our spiritual path and not an interruption, requires an entirely new mindset. It is necessary to be willing to see things differently and make new choices, to learn how to pray while punching a keyboard or turn paperwork into meditation. Once such a commitment is made, a sense of purpose emerges, putting a whole new spin on what we do. It starts to make everything count, gives zing to our routines, and, in fact, is capable of transforming those routines into expressions of conscious intention.

Richard Leider, business consultant and author of *The Power of Purpose*, considers purpose one's prime directive, the very reason one is born.

Purpose is that deepest dimension within us—our central core or essence—where we have a profound sense of who we are, where we came from, and where we're going . . . a discipline to be practiced day in and day out. . . . Purpose serves as the glue that holds the various aspects of our work together. It gives our work greater focus and energy. It serves as an inner guide by which we can judge appropriate responses to events, people, places, and time. Purpose is the passion that shapes our work life.

Purpose can come in large and small packages. I am "on purpose" as I write this chapter; you, dear reader, are on purpose as you read it, although what you may be seeking or learning is a mystery to all but yourself. We are on purpose whenever we take on a project or carry out a task, either at home or at work, personally or professionally. There doesn't always have to be an overt spiritual objective, of course (although for the enlightened among us, every act is a spiritual one). But in the big picture of our daily lives, it helps to have an anchor, a compelling reason to get up in the morning and, in this case, go to work. This is not simply a matter of changing attitudes but of overhauling previous motivations and replacing secular intentions with spiritual ones.

The Potential of Service

The most important of these intentions, I believe, is acting in the spirit of service, for anytime we are in service to another or to our community or to the Earth, we are doing the work of God. That's why those who are in the business of serving others, whether it be waiting tables or cutting hair or washing shirts, have the greatest potential for influencing the quality of our collective experience as human beings, one interaction at a time.

Rachel Naomi Remen, R.N.R., M.D., a pioneer in the mind-body health movement and author of *Kitchen Table Wisdom*, spoke beautifully about service in a talk she gave at a conference in San Diego. In it, she differentiated service from fixing or helping. When we are fixing, she says, it implies that something is broken. It's a form of judgment, separating the fixer from what—or who—is being fixed. "In fixing," she said, "there is an inequality of expertise that can easily become a moral distance. We cannot serve at a distance. We can only serve that to which we are profoundly connected, that which we are willing to touch. This [was] Mother Teresa's basic message. We serve life not because it is broken but because it is holy."

Helping, she feels, also implies inequality, and debt as well. It can mean that someone is needier than you are and that once helped, that person owes you, or feels that he does. Remen feels satisfaction when she helps but gratitude when she serves. "These are very different things," she says.

> *Service, on the other hand, is an experience of mystery, surrender, and awe. A fixer has the illusion of being causal. A server knows that he or she is being used and has a willingness to be used in the service of something greater, something essentially unknown. . . . From the perspective of service, we are all connected: All suffering is like my suffering and all joy is like my joy. The impulse to serve emerges naturally and inevitably from this way of seeing.*

Remen's beautiful portrayal of service honors the spirit of true community, one acknowledging that we're all in this together. At our workplaces, it would be no different; when *to give* becomes a central motivation in our work, we are honoring those around us and embracing them as fellow travelers. James M. Childs Jr. writes in his book *Ethics In Business: Faith at Work* that Jesus' teachings on service were no less than "revolutionary. For the Greeks, ruling was the truly fulfilling position to which one should aspire, not serving. Serving was considered undesirable and undignified. The service of the statesman to the state was honorable, but it was still thought of as self-fulfilling rather than an exercise in self-giving. For Jesus, service and servanthood are the marks of true discipleship and the traits that characterize his own person and work."

Those works included such admonitions as "whoever wishes to be great among you must be your servant, and whoever wishes to be first among you must be your slave," and the oft-cited symbolism of Jesus washing the feet of his disciples. "Jesus compares himself to one who serves at table rather than one who sits and is served," writes Childs, and indeed there are many who believe that Jesus was executed not because he was this Messiah person but because he championed those who, for whatever reason, were shunned—and perhaps feared—by the ruling elite.

And so, ironically, by placing service at the center of what we do, we become inadvertent role models for others. This marriage of service and leadership (however unintended) is remarkably similar to a contemporary theory and management practice that is growing in popularity. Called, not surprisingly, "servant-leadership," its most passionate advocate was a man named Robert Greenleaf. Greenleaf was a management professional and student of leadership models who was profoundly moved by Hesse's *Journey to the East*. The story convinced him that the mark of truly great leaders is the extent to which they truly serve others, and he founded an organization to further his ideas. In a seminal essay, "The Servant as Leader," he offered this definition of what makes a servant-leader.

> *It begins with the natural feeling that one wants to serve, to serve first. Then conscious choice brings one to aspire to lead. The difference manifests itself in the care*

taken by the servant-first to make sure that other people's highest-priority needs are being served.

The best test, and difficult to administer, is: do [those served] become healthier, wiser, freer, more autonomous, more likely themselves to become servants? And, what is the effect on the least privileged in society; will [they] benefit, or, at least, not be further deprived?

Greenleaf's emphasis on the value of leaders who put the needs of their employees, customers, and community above their own cannot be emphasized enough. Turning this notion on its head a bit and returning to an earlier observation, I would define a leader as anyone who has made selfless service a part of his work, regardless of whether he acknowledges such a role. This means that the cab driver who picks you up at the airport or the guy shining shoes on the sidewalk or the lady who vacuums the office floors at night could be living the kind of life that Jesus or Buddha or other ancient masters embodied.

Accept and Be Glad

Another key element in transforming our work from drudgery to sacred ground is acceptance, letting go and seeing it with new eyes. You consider yourself and your situation honestly, without judgment: This is a real job, with real people, that you have chosen to do. It may not be forever, but it is what you are doing now, in the present, which in most spiritual disciplines is the only moment that matters. Recall that whimsical proclamation, "Wherever you go, there you are." This saying is the closest thing that Western society has to a koan, the paradoxical riddles used in Zen Buddhism that help practitioners gain intuitive knowledge and reach deeper levels of meditation. It implies that where we are in life is the result of where we came from, but it also coaxes us to have presence of mind, to look not ahead or behind but at exactly where we are at the moment. Inside such awareness lie the keys to an expanded experience of what it means to be alive—really alive. There is a saying that the open hand can hold more sand than the clenched fist. When we are simply open to "what is," we find out that "what is" is a very interesting place.

Unfortunately, squeezed between quest and conquest, we've left ourselves little room for anything resembling acceptance; we're too caught up in the pictures we all have of what our ideal life *should* look like. We compare our lives with someone else's and strive for things that we've been taught to want and to use as measures of success. These slavish devotions take up valuable emotional and mental space, space that could be used in a much more productive way. If we instead poured such energy into our inner lives, the quality of our experience, no matter what our external conditions, would be vastly different. Satisfaction would start bubbling up from the inside with little provocation.

Part of the problem is that the idea of acceptance—outside of its obvious therapeutic benefits when applied to personal healing—has been misunderstood. Placed against the over-achieving architecture of Western economic culture, it does indeed have a hard time finding a home. But viewed from a larger perspective, its value becomes more apparent. Accepting your situation doesn't mean that you're resigned to it, nor is it an excuse to run away from problems or shrink from challenges. Rather, acceptance can be a way of saying yes to life and replacing damaging self-criticism with mindful self-evaluation.

Open Mind, Open Heart

In committing to making work part of our spiritual path, we prepare as we might for any important journey of discovery, and a good place to begin is with our attitude, our mental approach to the road ahead. In the classic book, *Zen Mind, Beginner's Mind*, Shunryu Suzuki-roshi talks about the importance of being open and curious, unattached to results or goals. The danger in being an expert, he warns, is that the field of possibilities is limited since the mind has already been crammed with answers; there's usually nowhere to go because the ground has already been covered. In a beginner's mind, however, everything is an adventure, a learning. An open mind can hold much more than a closed one. It's more versatile and responsive, bending but never breaking. Edmond Szekely, in *Creative Work: Karma Yoga*, writes about the importance of a proper attitude in the approach to work taken by those who practice the Hindu devotion of *karma yoga*.

> *In the highest sense, work is meant to be the servant of man, not the master. It is not so important what shape or form our work may take; what is vitally important is our attitude toward that work. With love and enthusiasm directed toward our work, what was once a chore and hardship now becomes a magical tool to develop, enrich and nourish our lives. 'Work makes the man' is an old proverb with much more truth in it than appears on the surface. Work can indeed make the man, if the man will use his God-given power of reason to transform work into the sacred partnership with the Creator it was originally meant to be.*

Cultivating such an attitude is a lifelong task, of course, but it's important to start somewhere, and every step, however small, takes us a little bit closer to enduring, fulfilling change. As you stand in front of your mirror in the morning—well, maybe after your first cup of coffee or herbal tea—take a moment to consider your attitude for the day. Is your heart open? Do you feel good about yourself? Do you know how important you are and how much impact your actions can have? Do you see your workplace as a classroom, even a cathedral? These questions can never be asked enough. There are so many distractions during the day, both from within and without, so many inertias of old attitudes and beliefs, that it's easy to get lost in old patterns of thinking. Forging new ones takes constant vigilance, but the effort, even one step at a time, pays off.

Starting the day this way doesn't have to be as sobering as it sounds. We don't have to leave our homes dressed in monkish garb, stone-faced with purpose. The path that we are taking—choosing—is ultimately one of joy and revelation. Indeed, one of the tools we can use is enthusiasm, energy, putting a bounce in our step. *Carpe diem!* is a masterstroke of motivation. The waitressing Margaret, for example, made her prework time count by turning it into a ritual that prepared her to seize her workplace.

> *Getting ready for work, I play my favorite music on the stereo, take a bath, and choose clothes to wear in which I feel comfortable and attractive. I decide how much money I want to make during my shift and visualize counting it at the end of the night. I expect to average at least 20 percent tips, and I usually get it! I also visualize having a good time with staff and customers.*

For others, this preparation may mean reading a good book on the morning subway commute or, if driving, listening to a favorite tape. The mode doesn't matter, only that we make an effort to cultivate a spirit of openness and self-awareness prior to arrival that creates inside ourselves the kind of space from which the best of work will be discovered.

Mindfulness

Nowhere in the study of conscious work can one not find mention of the value of mindfulness, the energy that helps us to "be here now" and approach our work as something more than a tedious obligation. It is from such an attentive state that we can begin to make meaningful contact with our workplace surroundings: the stress or joy in a co-worker's voice, the "feeling tone" of a room, our own inner landscape—the thoughts and emotions that color the hours of our days. Think about a recent day at work. Now try to recall some of the impressions you had about the people you worked with, met, or talked to that day. Does anything or anyone stand out—your boss, a co-worker, or a customer? Was there a particular conversation or exchange that could have been handled differently or that took you by surprise? How did you respond, and how could you have responded? In general, what can you learn about your workplace—such as office dynamics or certain personality styles—by reviewing it from this perspective? How will knowing these things help you in your job?

Mindfulness, of course, is an in-the-moment experience, a matter of training yourself to be aware. Reviewing the day in this way can start to sensitize our antennae until mindfulness grows into an active part of your work self. The world around you will begin to deepen as various levels of information start flowing in; you'll start to feel more connected and involved. Understanding the psycho-emotional architecture, the below-the-surface realities that may be motivating someone's behavior, also provides more options for how you can view a situation. It opens up other dimensions of experience that can help you choose more thoughtfully about how and when to respond, or even if a response is called for.

Essayist Jean Kinkead Martine, while working in an advertising agency, was keenly aware of the challenge in "seeing what is" and the gifts such a commitment might bring in an essay published in *Mindfulness and Meaningful Work*.

> *Perhaps it would be just in a daily lifelong attitude of "seeing" that the noisy, chaotic activity I call my job could become a support for my attention instead of a distraction. Perhaps, if I attend to the reality that is in front of me moment by moment—phone, pencil, boss, coffee—constantly failing, accepting to fail and to begin again—this perfectly ordinary work I do might become extraordinary work, might even become my craft.*

A perceptive waitress may observe subtle discontent coming from the new cook or the loneliness of the guy sipping coffee at the far table. A normally harried school bus driver would notice the boy with the sad eyes or the girl with the tattered skirt. Mindfulness can turn what might otherwise be just another blur in the chaos of our days into an opportunity for knowledge and compassionate response. It's the thing that makes what you do for a living more than just a job.

I recall a friend of mine, Lynn, telling me of a conversation that she had one afternoon with an overworked conference planner. She had called this person to verify a previous arrangement; the planner had been besieged by similar calls all morning and saw Lynn as just another irritating interruption. Lynn, noting the tension in the other woman's voice, said something like, "It sounds like you're having a bad day." The planner immediately softened. "You wouldn't believe it," she responded. Rather than a confrontation of attitudes, the two shared a pleasant few minutes and each went away feeling a little better. This was one of those small but unexpected moments of real contact that can make a tangible difference in someone's life. As Buddhist monk and author Thich Nhat Hanh reminds us,

"When the phone rings, take three deep breaths before answering it. You may never talk to that person again."

A job becomes a spiritual path not just when we start acknowledging the needs of others but also as we illuminate our own emotions and thoughts as we carry out our tasks. In the process of interacting with others and paying attention to what is happening, we begin to work out our own stuff *right there, right in the moment.* As in any intimate relationship where this level of commitment is made, our work lives become other mirrors for who we are. Such self-observation helps us to discover our strengths and weaknesses, our needs and frustrations, and the patterns that add to or subtract from the quality of our internal experiences.

Mindfulness helps us to see where in our work we get blocked as we seek to bring a higher quality of spirit and skill to our trade. It helps us to pay attention to our feelings when the person on the other end of the phone or sitting in the cab or paying for a pair of shoes treats us like day-old bread. In those moments of self-awareness, we can begin to slow things down, catch ourselves before an overreactive mind prompts us to say something that we later wish we hadn't. With mindfulness there also comes an element of detachment, which expands the space for seeing things from a broader perspective. Freed from the pestering voices of our own insecurities, we can start to choose different responses and take more control over our experiences. As we integrate this skill into our work lives, everything shifts. We deepen our relationships to those around us because we are responding from a deeper, clearer place.

Roshi Philip Kapleau writes about the interplay of mindfulness and work in his book *The Three Pillars of Zen.* Focusing on manual labor in particular—sweeping, dusting, cleaning, and gardening—he notes the object of such work.

[It is] the cultivation first of mindfulness and eventually of mindlessness. [Mindfulness is defined as awareness in which one is aware that one is aware; mindlessness is a condition of complete absorption beyond any self-awareness.] All labor entered into with such a mind is valued for itself apart from what it may lead to. . . . By understanding each task in this spirit, eventually we are enabled to grasp the truth that every act is an expression of the Buddha-mind. Once this is directly and unmistakably experienced, no labor can be beneath one's dignity. On the contrary, all work, no matter how menial, is ennobling.

7

Start from Where You Are

Nothing great is created suddenly, any more than a bunch of grapes or a fig. If you tell me that you desire a fig, I answer that there must be time. Let it first blossom, then bear fruit, then ripen.

—*Epictetus*

As we face our daily work, committed to making it a tool for spiritual growth, we accept that where we are is the perfect place to start and realize that service is the touchstone that will ground our daily actions. In taking such a journey, we will discover more of our gifts and talents than we ever thought we had as we are challenged to be our best. And challenged we will be, for the workplace—almost any workplace—provides a wealth of opportunities to exercise our spiritual muscles. Consider a day in the life of a "typical" school bus driver from *Flight of the Phoenix* by John Whiteside and Sandra Egli.

"In school districts across the nation, bus drivers pick up children in the morning and get them home safely each day. It is not an easy job. There are medically fragile students to assist and violent children to restrain. Angry motorists, resentful at waiting for the school bus to load or unload, sometimes make obscene gestures or brandish firearms. The drivers see children who are sad, suffering, and poor. They have been known to use their own funds to buy mittens, hats, and even coats for the children who have none."

As you consider the description above, think of all the qualities that are required to do this job well: compassion and patience, diplomacy and strength, generosity and sensitivity, and healthy self-esteem, none of which are strangers to the spiritual path. Who would have thought that driving a school bus would provide so many opportunities to exercise one's spiritual potential? Think of your own workplace. Take a single day, or even a single hour, and go through it minute by minute. Make a list of everything you do, from the simplest task to the most challenging. Leave nothing out. For some of you, this exercise will be relatively simple; for others, it may be more complicated. Consider the following example for those who wait tables, taken from a training seminar outline. You may think you know what waiting tables is like based on what you've seen as a customer—lots of smiling, speedwalking, and juggling—but there's a whole lot more to it, not to mention what lurks between the lines.

- Preparing the work station
- Setting the table
- Initiating service
- Taking orders
- Rules for different table types (standing, booth, banquet)
- Communicating with the cooks
- Pacing the meal
- Service priorities
- Tray-loading techniques

- Tray rotation
- Splitting items
- Condiments and sauces
- Writing checks.
- Clearing the table
- Guest relations ("reading" guests, developing rapport, describing the menu, making suggestions)
- Handling complaints

As you take a closer look at your own workplace, you'll probably be surprised at everything it takes to do your job well. Use the questions below as a guide. Start in the morning and follow your workday until you walk out the door.

1. Does your work involve building, repairing, or cleaning? Paperwork? Computers? Telephones? How would you describe what you do—in detail—to others?
2. What do you actually provide in terms of a service or product? Who is it for? Businesses, individuals, or the general community? How is your product or service used and/or appreciated? Who benefits from what you do? What purpose is being served?
3. Do you work with others? Customers, fellow employees? What do you talk about? Do you mostly instruct, listen, guide, console, or report?

Everyone's list will be different, of course; the point is to first become aware of what it is that we actually do at work. With that knowledge, we begin to see that what we think is an endless series of busy—although essentially empty— hours leading to an exhausting conclusion is in fact a treasure chest of openings for manifesting our spiritual selves. This is where purpose comes in. Are our actions meeting the needs of others in just a functional way—delivering the food on time or transporting the children safely—or do they reflect a broader vision? Purpose with a small "p"—going that extra step, looking for opportunities to serve—follows from Purpose with a capital "P"—the commitment that we have made to use our work as a means of spiritual expression and growth.

As we saw in the tradition of *Chado* (The Way of Tea) and the tea ceremony, purpose and intention are used to create harmony of atmosphere that can "ennoble" others to experience something out of the ordinary even in the most ordinary of settings. By seeing in our own work the same possibilities, we begin to participate in a revolution of spirit that can slowly transform the sameness of our days into a purposeful search for meaning and personal growth. As we bring new energy to our work, the work itself begins to reward our effort, becoming both our teacher and our teaching.

Tarthang Tulku, who introduced the Buddhist idea of "skillful means" to the West, wrote, "When we rely on work as our practice, we get direct, immediate feedback that is remarkably useful on any kind of spiritual path. . . . The steady challenges of work force us to develop more knowledge. We cut through the paralyzing sense that time spent working is time taken away from our real concerns and interest and win back control over half our lives."

It's not just a matter of making a job more interesting or more bearable, although this will be a natural outcome of such an effort. It's also about making it part of who we are and how we want to impact the world we live in. Essayist Jean Kinkead Martine once lamented that "in my usual way of working I feel nothing precarious or risky. Nothing is really at stake." What I'm talking about here is the very opposite of that: making work risky again, where *everything* is at stake. This elevates every moment to a potentially transformative one: for you, for your work, and for the person whom you touch with unexpected heart. Sometimes the transformations will be so small as to be unnoticeable; at other times they'll bring a smile to your face or lightness to your walk, or you may simply become quiet and feel a shift in your depths.

Through the Front Door

The real work begins with the first phone call in the morning or the first customer or the first indelicate command from a superior. Maybe it's discovering that someone on the night shift left your work station a mess. Sometimes it's nothing more than simply being confronted with that familiar complex of thought forms—the mindset—that makes up the predominant attitude of a particular workplace, from starched white-collar conservatism to bureaucratic lethargy and everything in between. It's hard not to succumb to their influence. I can remember walking through the doors of the casino where I worked and feeling as if I were suddenly swimming against a strong current; the psychic ocean was thick with its own personality, its own motivations and emotions. Before I learned how to transmute those energies, I would simply be swept away as my individual personality surrendered to the collective swirl.

Whatever the circumstances, your "job" is beginning, and you will need to start exercising the skills and using the tools that will bring a spiritual dimension to what you do. At this point, there are a couple of important things to keep in mind.

- Know that what you do is needed in the world (even if it is sometimes unappreciated).
- Your purpose is to be of service and *to learn*.
  Nearly everything that you do at work will present you with both of these opportunities.
- You aren't pursuing a goal as much as creating a process.

In winding the spiritual path through our workplaces, we need to continually remind ourselves that while startling and unexpected shifts in perception do happen—moments of sudden clarity, a modest epiphany—we aren't in a race; spiritual growth is a gradual process. Change will come—sometimes slowly, sometimes in great gulps—but the rate is far less important than the fact that a commitment has been made.

There will be lots of ups and downs, plenty of encouragement to demean what we do or the company we work for and to participate in conspiracies of discontent. But as long as we remember the purpose and mission, as long as we stay open and cultivate a loving attitude, there will always be a place to go when work begins to befuddle us. As we change, as our work begins to feed the hunger of our souls, we will know in the very marrow of our bones that the effort has been worth it.

One way to start is to take a single day and turn it into an experiment. Decide to focus on one thing, say, detachment. Not detachment that takes you away from caring about what's happening but one that gives you permission to maintain emotional distance from any kind of drama, such as your supervisor's bad day or a customer who decides to take everything out on you. In other words, try to be in the world but not of it.

During this day, make a mental note of what is happening inside you or write down your impressions during private time. How does it feel to be in such a state? How are people responding to you? When you find yourself getting sucked in, gently remind yourself to adjust your attitude. It will be difficult at times, especially when your particular buttons are being pushed, but that's okay. Look at the experience as exploratory research. You can pick almost any quality that you aspire to—patience, enthusiasm, honesty, curiosity, kindness, or even joy—and try it on for a day. What you'll find surprising in this process is the effect that even the smallest changes can have and how even the most difficult of jobs can be transformed by slight shifts in perspective.

One story in particular that impressed me concerned phone operators at AT&T. This oft-maligned group labors under ceaseless pressure while fighting boredom, repetition, and lots of disgruntled callers. It has been estimated that each operator handles about 700 calls a day, one right after the other, with little or no time to prepare for the next question or complaint or to recover from the previous one. At the same time, that voice on the other end of the line that helps us to navigate through the telephonic universe can have quite a bit of impact, even for the brief period of time that we are in contact with it. Even my last sentence is evidence of what these folks put up with sometimes, disembodying them as I did by using the word *it* to describe their existence. So the challenges are clear, and it's usually no mystery to us which operators are up to those challenges and which ones are merely punching a time card.

Some years ago, Timothy Gallwey, author of *The Inner Game of Tennis* and other similarly titled books, was brought in by AT&T to help make the operators' jobs "less threatening and more interesting." Gallwey's basic game plan was to help them control their experiences by teaching them to pay closer attention to each caller, identifying the caller's mood, and imagining what they might look like. Essentially, he was asking them to humanize the people at the other end of the line, which is something that all of us should keep in mind. He also suggested that they use an awareness technique of evaluating those voices moment by moment and then assigning a number to the intensity of the emotion they were hearing, such as Angry 4, Angry 8, and so on. The results of this simple technique turned out to be many-fold.

- They "changed the game" by adding a task that wasn't directly related to the business at hand. As a result, they altered potentially disruptive exchanges by perceiving a caller's anger not as a personal attack but as something simply to be aware of. In so doing, they were able to keep their own emotions out of it and resolve the issue more effectively.
- By keeping their cool, they helped to defuse the caller's frustration level.
- By humanizing the experience and adding the element of control, boredom and stress levels were reduced, and the job became more interesting.

Was this a spiritual transformation? Maybe not in a grand sense, but compassion and respect were introduced into a situation in which there was little or none of it, and therein lies the power of what took place.

Mining the Gold

In many respects, mining the spirituality in our work is not so different from just "being a good person" or "doing a good job," expressing such qualities as patience, enthusiasm, attentiveness, responsibility, humility, and skillful performance. It's doing unto others as you would have others do unto you.

But too often in our rush to the twenty-first century, we've allowed these values to atrophy in importance, or we've simply forgotten them altogether. When we encounter another person—often when we least expect it—who is living them out, we're struck by how refreshing it feels and how touched we are by such contact.

Spirituality is thus made real when it can be felt in a tangible way. Yes, the devil is in the details, but so is God. In fact, it's this dance of apparent opposites that can create the miracle of transformation: Tedium can lead to mindfulness, anger can bring out compassion, and irritation can give birth to patience. In doing any job well, with purpose and caring, we are showing respect for those who will benefit from it, respect for the job itself, and belief in our own self-worth.

No one says that this will be easy. It's not enough that we simply choose to make service a spiritual path; we must then confront what it will take to walk it, facing our own as well as others' demons. Although a number of tools have been offered to assist you on this journey, all the mindfulness in the world won't do much good when your head is throbbing, the guy in front of you has three-day-old breath, and your job appraisal starts in 30 minutes. The challenge of putting another's need ahead of your own can create tension that is often difficult to overcome. We must be willing to give even when we don't feel like giving and honor others even when they don't seem to deserve it.

We will wrestle our prejudices and flee from our weaknesses. Perhaps we'll discover that we're lazier than we thought or that envy has camped out on our good intentions. Our "shadow sides" will inevitably leak—or surge—out: the pettiness, the anger, the jealousy, and the impatience. We'll fight indifference, distraction, insensitivity, and despair. The inertia of the status quo will resist us at every step—not just the job itself, but what is happening in our minds. The urge to run screaming from our workplaces will suddenly begin to look pretty good.

Times like these are unavoidable. They push us to the limit and test our resolve. We will stumble, of course, and grope blindly in the dark. But as long as our purpose remains steadfast, as long as we remember that this is a lifelong process and that new opportunities will arise at any moment, we will at least stumble *forward*.

There is an old Jewish folktale about two businessmen who lived in a small town. The one with a good heart and a kind word for those around him was quite successful; the other, plagued by a sour disposition and prone to resentment and insecurity, was not. One day, the unsuccessful one asked the other if he would be willing to start a business with him. The successful merchant, wanting to help his less fortunate acquaintance, agreed. Well, the arrangement quickly went sour, as the good shopkeeper was somehow cheated by his new partner. Broke and disgraced, with no way to support his family, he was forced to seek work in a foreign land, where he spent long, fruitless days of searching. Finally, when he was about to give up, an innkeeper hired him as a waiter.

Grateful to have found work, he applied himself selflessly to his task, attracting the attention of the owner, who gave him another responsibility: filling three water jugs every night. This he agreed to do, but to his puzzlement, one of them was always empty in the morning. One night, he stayed awake to find out what was happening, and sure enough, he saw a great eagle swoop down from the heavens and grab one of the containers with its mighty talons. Some time later, the eagle returned it, empty.

The following night, the waiter grabbed the jar and the eagle carried him to its nest on a distant mountain. There he saw that the water was for the eagle's newly hatched babies, because there was no water in that high place. He also noticed that the mountaintop was strewn with gold nuggets. He filled his pockets with them, and then the eagle carried him back to the inn. He informed the owner that it was time for him to go home, returned to his family with his newfound wealth, paid his debts, and restored his good name.

In the meantime, the cheating shopkeeper was having his troubles, and he asked his formerly disgraced partner how he managed to become so wealthy. The compassionate merchant, who was still willing to help this poor fellow, told him the story. "I will even write to my former employer, recommending you if you'd like," he said, willing to let bygones be bygones. Satisfied by the good merchant's recommendation, the innkeeper hired the man and gave him the same responsibilities.

That very night, he saw the eagle carry away the jug. The next night he hopped a ride, then eagerly stuffed his pockets with the nuggets. But they turned out to be hot coals! Covered with burns and with nowhere to go, he wandered off in despair.

After a while, the restaurant owner wrote a letter to the honest shopkeeper, telling him about the man's disappearance. When it became clear that the ill-intentioned merchant would not return, the shopkeeper set up a pension for the bereft wife and her children and took care of them as well as his own family.

The merchant's discovery of the gold was not an end in itself; it was a grace that came to him after a difficult time during which he carried himself with dignity and acted honorably. In fact, his continued generosity and commitment to selfless service despite sudden—and unfair—setbacks was his true wealth. Ironically, it was this devotion *without expectation of reward* that ultimately brought him material comfort as well. The story tells us that being true to a higher intention inevitably guarantees that all other needs will be met, for this is the way of the universe. "Set thy heart upon thy work, but never on its reward," instructs the *Bhagavad Gita*. "When work is done as sacred work, unselfishly, with a peaceful mind, without lust or hate, with no desire for reward, then the work is pure."

So when our work world is coming down on our heads, it's helpful to take a moment and carefully choose how to respond. This literally happened to me the summer after my freshman year in college. Through a temp agency, I found work on a small construction project, joining three other guys on an experienced crew: the foreman, 60 years old, with a steady hand and a good eye; an amusing chain-smoker with tattoos on his arms who reminded me of comedian George Carlin; and a bear of a man who had room for a keg of beer in his stomach.

To make a long story short, the big guy didn't like this greenhorn college boy, not one bit. One afternoon, after days of making this very clear, he dropped a one-inch bolt directly on my head from atop a 20-foot-high wall while I sat cross-legged on the ground below, hammering nails. The pain was instantaneous, followed quickly by humiliation as he mumbled a lame apology. It was the final blow to my spirit. I sat for a long moment, recovering from the shock and struggling to figure out what to do. I finally decided to do nothing, to "endure with dignity" and keep on hammering. Nothing more was said about the incident. Maybe he felt sorry for me or was somehow moved by my voiceless response. Whatever the reason, something in him changed, and from that day on he treated me with respect. To my 17-year-old mind, I had moved a mountain.

Everyone has such stories, tales of difficult bosses or quarrelsome co-workers or feeling trapped in a situation over which they had little control. In facing these challenges and striving to resolve them by means of spiritual tools, we start building the character that makes us whole while bringing meaning to what we do. It's an empowering process, made especially so by the fact that conscious choices are driving it. Indeed, the "spiritualizing" of our work proceeds to the extent that we ourselves become spiritualized, integrating our highest values into what we do and using work as a teacher and as a mirror. Tarthang Tulku speaks of "disciplined work" as an actual practice in which awareness, concentration, and energy are the three primary tools. He correlates with awareness such qualities as being respectful, precise, vigilant, receptive, and subtle; concentration brings forward engagement, contemplation, intent, persistence, and devotion; energetic people are vigorous, enthusiastic, warm, inspiring, and effective.

Keeping up our energy is especially challenging when work feels like nothing more than tedium and repetition; no one is immune to such forces. And yet, at times like this, we should ask ourselves this question: Is it the work itself that is lacking in energy, or our approach to it? There are very few jobs that can't be made more lively and creative. One example concerns an inventive traffic cop who put a refreshing face on the stereotype of rigid men in blue.

A massive construction site near my old office in Seattle, where a spectacular new office building was under way, had been distracting drivers to the point where accidents were happening and traffic was consistently snarled. For days, a frustrated policeman did his best to keep things moving, but nothing seemed to work. No matter how many times he whistled or vigorously shook his baton, the gawkers and the chaos of dump trucks and cranes conspired to make a mess of things. Then one day, he appeared on the job as a different person. He was animated and engaged, waving his arms and doing moves like Michael Jackson. Using his baton like a magic wand, he became the most entertaining show around. His energy was like a magnet, drawing people's attention away from the rising girders nearby. By the force of his will but with a decidedly light touch, he transformed that congested intersection into a smoothly flowing artery. And he also changed himself. He stepped out of the box of his normal routine. The impact that his new attitude had was many-fold; it may even have saved a life.

Here on the island where I now live, the only way in or out is by boat. Several times a day, a ferry from the mainland (or "America," as we affectionately call it) slides into port, discharges its cargo, and loads up for the return trip. There is always a handful of "ferry people," stationed both on the boat and off, who orchestrate this vehicular ritual as waiting cars descend from an uphill parking lot. Their role is not unlike that of the traffic cop, making sure that everyone goes in the right direction at the right time with a minimum of confusion and time lost. Sometimes there's a little bit of explaining to do ("Why is the ferry so late?"), and sometimes moral support is needed. This is especially important during the busy summer months, when first-time visitors may wait for hours for the next boat, fighting boredom, anxiety, and restless children.

Normally, we don't pay much attention to the *who* of this process, but one guy in particular can't help but be noticed. Maybe it's the way he looks—a bushy mustache, ruddy cheeks, eyes that seem to sparkle under his cap, and those teeth, always big and white behind a smile that never stops. Weather doesn't seem to deter him, no matter how hot, wet, or blustery. He has become the de facto official greeter for those who have just arrived ("My, what a friendly place") and someone to whom you want to doff your hat as you roll down toward the boat. What makes such a guy tick?

"I enjoy people," he explains in a decidedly jolly tone. "I like helping them, fixing their problems. When you lighten things up, people will respond. Humor and courtesy go a long way. The key is attitude; it takes a lot less energy to be positive than negative." When asked if people get on his nerves, he answers, "Not very often. The whole ferry thing is very emotional: people frantic to get on, frustrated when they don't, lots of early mornings and long days. It's ripe for confrontation. If I can reduce at least some of their stress, all the better. A lot of it is listening and being empathetic. You can't always work miracles, but you can try."

Such thoughtful and enthusiastic engagement not only makes any job more fun for the one doing it but also lightens the load of anyone whom that job touches. This is another way that work can serve us, by motivating us to be more involved, to keep our energy moving and replenished. Such efforts can't help but carry over into the rest of our lives.

Tarthang Tulku writes that by making our work a training in the qualities showcased above, "we test our understanding, our commitment, and our willingness to take responsibility. These qualities have always been necessary for spiritual development; what we are doing is putting them at the center of our practice in a new way. That is the level at which we aim to practice skillful means."

In her own way, Margaret, the waitress we met in the preceding chapter, applies skillful means to her job as a waitress. From the silverware to the service, she attends to everything in her job with the same spirit of importance.

> *At the restaurant, I make sure my station is impeccable—table settings in order, napkins folded just so, the bus station organized so that I feel supported. I even tape the daily crossword puzzle on the station wall so that we can have fun during the lulls. I sample the evening's special so that I can rave about it (or not!). I've learned to memorize orders, even for tables of up to six. It's a challenge, but I know my customers are usually impressed. If I forget a customer's name, I make a game of it by imagining their partner calling it out when I'm at the table. It usually works! If anything goes wrong (I mess up an order, the kitchen is slow), I make sure that it's handled in a way that everyone is taken into consideration, from the customer to the busboy. I feel that the customers are coming into my home, so I make sure they feel nurtured, that they are in a place of beauty. The owners believe that buying customers an occasional drink or dessert can be good for business.*

Whether or not she is consciously aware of it, Margaret has internalized the following principles of "customership" that I found on the Internet, courtesy of someone known only as the Wok Warrior.

- A customer is not dependent on us; we are dependent on him.
- A customer is not an interruption of our work; he is the purpose of our work.
- A customer does us a favor when he calls; we are not doing him a favor by serving him.
- A customer is a vital part of our business, not an outsider.
- A customer is not a cold statistic; he is a flesh-and-blood human being with feelings and emotions just like our own.
- A customer is not someone to argue with but someone to help.
- A customer is a person who brings us his needs, and it is our job to fill those needs.
- A customer is deserving of the most courteous and attentive treatment we can give him.
- A customer is the most important person in any business.

Imagine what it would feel like to walk into a restaurant in which everyone had the same intention and carried the same spirit as Margaret, where the above list was not just a bunch of empty definitions but universal laws. It's when work is approached with such a purpose that it becomes a spiritual path. Being good at and feeling fulfilled by what we do is not so much about achieving perfection or even about having the right attitude but about being real and bringing all of our senses to bear on what we are doing, leaving nothing out. "Many men go fishing all their lives," Thoreau once wrote, "without knowing that it is not fish they are after."

The service that we provide as part of the work we do—no matter what kind or with whom—can start to honor the web of life that we are all a part of, human and nonhuman. In the case of waiting tables, for example, the serving of food can become a ritual, a ceremony, that connects us to each other and each person to himself. An ambiance can be created that, even during the blue-light special, resonates with life-giving energy. Our movements begin having a seamlessness and grace. The boundaries between who we are and what we do dissolve as the activity itself provides the means for opening up to spirit.

Everything is interconnected, and thus, everything we do counts. (I can't help but think of that popular notion among chaos-theory enthusiasts suggesting that the flutter of a butterfly's wings in your own backyard can affect the weather patterns a continent away.) Any aspect of work, then, no matter how menial, is imbued with sacred potential. If we come to that work with the conscious intention of making it part of our spiritual path, of honoring its place in the vast web of events and relationships that make up our sensory world, a transformation must take place.

Making Space Count

An often-neglected part of our jobs is the physical environment and the tools of our trades. Keeping the work area organized and pleasant and caring for the instruments that we use brings an element of beauty into our work lives. In so many societies, physical objects aren't given the respect that they deserve. Especially in this country, we are a culture that too often thinks in terms of new and improved, not old and reliable. Things are made to be used and abused, then discarded and replaced. We've lost contact with the craftsmanship that goes into the making of the tools of our various trades, even something as simple as a pen or a brush or a pair of scissors. It's true that many of them are the products of mass production, but often it's the energy that we put into them that can raise them from "necessary things" to valuable friends.

In the casinos, with so much standing and walking, a carefully tended pair of shoes could make all the difference between a long, painful night and a relatively comfortable one. Even a cook's simple spatula—how much better it is to keep it from becoming a dark, oil-encrusted club.

Am I showing a compulsive nature here? I hope not. "Cleanliness is next to godliness" is an overused phrase—one that echoes from my childhood—but there's truth in what it suggests: that heaven looks kindly on those who take care of the material things in their lives, for aren't these also of the spirit? If one believes that the energy of the universe that pulsates in our bodies is found in physical objects as well, then it makes perfect sense to extend appropriate respect. Those who perform the Japanese tea ceremony take great care in the way that the various items of the actual ceremony are chosen, used, and maintained. In the book *Illusions: The Adventures of a Reluctant Messiah*, the bush pilot takes care of his plane's engine so it never fails, and in the cult classic *Zen and the Art of Motorcycle Maintenance*, the protagonist is at one with his bike because, among other things, he has devoted himself to its inner workings. Both of these characters know, like the masters of the Japanese tea ceremony, that God can be found just as easily under the hood of a car as on a mountain peak or within the bud of a rose.

There's another Japanese approach to organizing the workplace that, although it doesn't have the sacred tradition of the tea ceremony behind it, nevertheless can call into play a host of virtuous activities. It's called 5S, which stands for *seiri* (simplify), *seiton* (straighten), *seiso* (scrub), *seiketsu* (stabilize), and *shitsuke* (sustain). The practice, originating in Japanese manufacturing and agriculture, is used by a number of major corporations and is usually a precursor of more fundamental policy changes. The implication is that if people cannot do something as simple as keep their workplaces clean, how can they take on more serious initiatives? Clutter begets clutter, they seem to be saying, internally as well as externally. Beyond the aesthetic focus of this process, which adherents claim can improve worker morale and productivity and motivate loyal customers, there is also an attitudinal element. In fact, how clean things are is secondary to having the right attitude about the cleaning. It shouldn't be duty that compels but a sense of rightness, a knowledge that to care for our work environments in such a fashion is to honor what we do.

Finally, we rarely hear the words *job* and *altar* in the same breath, but the notion of turning any physical space, including where we work, into a personal altar is gaining in popularity. Not *altar* in a traditional sense, but as a reminder that our spiritual needs should be tended, no matter where we find ourselves. Creating sacred space at work can also help us stay anchored in the values that we want to express while we're on the job. Full-blown ornaments such as life-size Buddhas or sun-scorched animal skulls or incense burners and the like may not always be appropriate, and not all spaces are conducive to divine design, but even something as simple as fresh flowers, a favorite saying, a special photograph, or a cherished stone can make a difference. The goal is to use these items as touchstones for staying centered on who you want to be as the demands of the day conspire to knock you off-course.

The attentiveness that we direct to the physical characteristics of our workspaces can't help but affect the "how" of what we do. Having spent the extra time making sure that our tools are cared for, the floor is swept, or the pencils are sharpened, we are that much more attuned to the quality of our own performances. This will elevate our relationships to our jobs by widening the sphere of what we value. As our connection to the work strengthens, we start seeing it as more of a craft than a job, and our commitment to it deepens.

8

We All Carry Trays

*There was a young man named Trotaka
who did the laundry for the great sages. He
did his job well, without complaint, but he
was ignored by the sages because he was from
a lower caste. One day, while these great men
prepared to chant an important hymn, a
song more beautiful than anything they had
ever heard soared from the river. "What can
that be?" the sages asked. They rushed to the
river to find the source of the magnificent
sound. And there was Trotaka. In doing
simple things without thought of reward or
recognition, Trotaka had become enlightened.*
—ADAPTED FROM THE UPANISHADS

This wonderful parable gives me the opportunity to
again invoke my favorite twentieth-century expression, Catch-
22, which summed up the absurdities of the war for the over-
rational Yossarian in Joseph Heller's 1961 book of the same
name. In the story above, we have the greatest minds in the
world studying the great scriptures and singing the great songs
in hopes of attaining the great something that cannot be at-

tained by such a process. Trotaka was not after enlightenment; he was merely being himself, embodied in his selfless washing of the sages' clothes. This purity of spirit, however, this at-one-(mo)ment with his task, brought forth from within him the most glorious song of the universe.

When we are in harmony with ourselves and the people and things around us, we will also sing such a song, and it will be heard by anyone who takes the time to listen. Such are the possibilities in the workplace, no matter what kind of work we do. This doesn't mean that we shouldn't fight for what's fair or that we can't leave a situation that is impossible to endure. It does mean that for most of us, the labors of our days have tremendous potential as agents of transformation, not so much in terms of the macrocosmic impact of visionary corporate policies (which nevertheless are much needed) but in the intimate, day-to-day interactions that have real and immediate meaning.

In *The Turning Point*, Fritjof Capra wrote about what he perceived as two kinds of work. The first kind, usually the more glamorized, has to do with creating things that last: buildings, planes, highways, "products of high technology." The other kind, entropic work, is the work of repetition whose impact is short-lived, like that of the cook or the bank teller or the hotel clerk, whose customers will keep coming back, day after day, for food or money or rest. Such work, says Capra, actually connects one to the deeper spiritual rhythms of life.

> *Doing work that has to be done over and over again helps us to recognize the natural cycles of growth and decay, of birth and death, and thus become aware of the dynamic order of the universe . . . and . . . will allow us to recapture its spiritual essence.*

Capra speaks to the institutional and philosophical need to revalue work, to bring it more in line with how the ancient canons of religious tradition perceived its place in the human universe. Such a dialogue is sorely needed. At the same time, the resacralizing of work will more than likely be a bottom-up process, as individuals awaken to the largely dormant capacities of work to change them at a fundamental level. This door is open to anyone. No degrees are needed, no expensive spiritual training is required, just a willingness to include work in the commitment to live a more conscious life and recognition that the work you do can and does make a difference. What's at stake when such a choice is made?

- Empowerment through decisiveness: When we resolve to do things differently, to stretch ourselves outside the familiar, the fear we experience is often tempered by exhilaration. This is our soul's way of saying "Thank you." Blaming someone or something else for our troubles will only keep us in whatever trouble we think we're in. When we take responsibility, we start taking control.
- Using power appropriately: Yes, we all have power, the ability to influence people or events, even in small ways. By bringing consciousness into our workplaces, we are using our power as a force for good.
- Respect for ourselves and respect for others: In making our work spiritual, we are showing that we care about who we want to be in this life. And by acknowledging the essential value and basic goodness of others, we are honoring their own unique spirits. Like begets like, and when we treat others with kindness and compassion, we are that much more likely to get the same in return.
- Interconnectedness: That society has become fragmented, that we have largely cut ourselves off from

meaningful relationships with the world around us, is an unfortunate fact of modern times. When our work becomes part of our spiritual paths, however, we begin to rebuild those connections and restore to health the web of which we are all a part.

- Accepting and honoring what is; living in the moment: I suspect that many of us have spent too much of our lives regretting yesterday or fearing tomorrow, which hasn't done a lot for today. A commitment to "spiritual work" asks us to focus on the present, to pour ourselves into it as if it's the only moment that counts (which most mystics will tell you is absolutely true). In so doing, old wounds will start to heal and the future will become much less intimidating.

- A lifetime of learning: Mildred Ryder, the Peace Pilgrim, who spread her message of peace as she walked across the United States, once said that life "is a school where people will eventually develop into the image and likeness of God." How can—or does—our work help us on such a path? What lessons does it bring? Patience, understanding, laughter, and love? When work is made spiritual, everyone we contact and everything that happens becomes a teacher.

Nasreen Koaser is a beautiful example of this. A hairstylist who arrived in the United States from India, she at first had trouble adapting to her new home, to its customs and culture. This sparked a period of deep reflection that, as Richard Leider recalls in *The Power of Purpose*, "caused her to go deep inside to discover the true nature of herself and her work." What she found—a powerful desire to share her core self with others—should inspire anyone who questions the transformative power of their own labors. Because she brings pure love to her work, people come from all around, and her calendar is filled for months in advance. She greets each client with hot tea, a kind word, a smile, and a touch. She says, "I love my work because I love my clients. Every day God gives me the opportunity to bring out the pure essence in my clients. That is my purpose, and I am grateful for work that allows me to use my gifts in this way."

We all have special gifts that we bring to our workplaces, and we all have work that can help us to express—and discover—those gifts. The kind of service and devotion discussed in this book and embodied by Koaser and others shows that the marriage of work and spirituality is not only possible but already alive in the world, providing a haven for those being served and nurturing the spirit of those who serve. Turning our work into a spiritual practice will provide context and meaning to what otherwise can feel like an isolated and spiritless task. It will connect us to the world at a meaningful level and bring about congruency between our inner longings and our outer realities. The boundaries between who we are, what we do, and when and where we do it will begin to dissolve. Our lives will become more whole.

We all carry trays, for everything we do can be an act of service. Recall that old saying, "If you meet the Buddha in the middle of the road, kill him." During a time of intense spiritual searching and dime-store, self-aggrandizing gurus, it cautioned against looking outside ourselves for answers. That caution still has value, but when we honor at work the Buddha-like potential in those around us with our thoughts and our actions, we are participants in a revolution in consciousness.

In the mad rush that is life, be it family, work, social, or otherwise, it's easy to forget that we share this planet with other human beings who are very much like we are. When we interact with others, do we make a difference in their lives?

What kind of difference? Do we ennoble others, or do we pass them by as if they were cardboard figures on a stage?

Perhaps the most important thing anyone can ask themselves is, Why am I here; what is my purpose? What does it mean in the realm of the day-to-day: at work, when traveling, with friends and loved ones? Everything we do, every moment we breathe, counts. How will we spend this time? Are we adding to the sum total of goodness in the world?

We all carry trays because we are not alone on this earth, and the web of life is a fragile one. It's important that we take care of it.

Matthew Gilbert

References and
Recommended Reading

Bellman, Geoffrey M. *Your Signature Path: Gaining New Perspectives on Life and Work.* San Francisco: Berrett-Koehler, 1996.

Briskin, Alan. *The Stirring of Soul in the Workplace.* San Francisco: Jossey-Bass, 1996.

Castille, Rand. *The Way of Tea.* New York: Weatherhill, 1971.

Childs, James M. Jr. *Ethics in Business: Faith at Work.* Minneapolis: Augsburg Fortress, 1995.

Cowan, John. *The Common Table: Reflections and Meditations on Community and Spirituality in the Workplace.* New York: HarperBusiness, 1993.

Egli, Sandra and John Whiteside. *Flight of the Phoenix: Soaring to Success in the 21st Century.* Newton, MA: Butterworth-Heinemann, 1996.

Eknath, Easwaran. *Gandhi the Man: The Story of His Transformation.* Tomales, Calif.: Nilgiri Press, 1997.

Fox, Matthew. *The Reinvention of Work: A New Vision of Livelihood for Our Time.* New York: Harper San Francisco, 1994.

Kaye, Les. *Zen at Work: A Zen Teacher's 30-Year Journey in Corporate America.* New York: Random House, 1996.

Leider, Richard. *The Power of Purpose*. San Francisco: Berrett-Koehler, 1997.

Moran, Victoria. *Shelter for the Spirit: How to Make Your Home a Haven in a Hectic World*. New York: HarperCollins, 1996.

Richards, Dick. *Artful Work: Awakening Joy, Meaning, and Commitment in the Workplace*. San Francisco: Berrett-Koehler, 1995.

Schumacher, E. F. *Small Is Beautiful: Economics As If People Mattered* New York: Harper & Row, 1973.

Sen XV, Soshitsu. *Tea Life, Tea Mind*. New York: Weatherhill 1979.

Sinetar, Marsha. *Do What You Love, The Money Will Follow*. Mawah, NJ: Paulist Press, 1987.

Snyder, Don J. *The Cliff Walk: A Memoir of a Job Lost and a Life Found*. Boston: Little, Brown, 1997.

Stackhouse, Max L. and Dennis P. McCann, editors; Shirley J. Roels, Preston N. Williams. *On Moral Business: Classical and Contemporary Resources for Ethics in Economic Life*. Grand Rapids, MI: Eerdmans Publishing, 1995.

Taylor, Daniel. *The Healing Power of Stories: Creating Yourself through the Stories of Your Life*. New York: Doubleday, 1996.

Terkel, Studs. *Working*. New York: Ballantine, 1985.

Tulku, Tarthang. *Mastering Successful Work*. Berkeley: Dharma Publishing, 1994.

Vitell, Bettina. *The World in a Bowl of Tea*. New York: Harper-Collins, 1997.

Whitmyer, Claude, ed. *Mindfulness and Meaningful Work: Explorations in Right Livelihood*. New York: Parallax Press, 1994.

Williams, Oliver and John Houck. *The Judeo-Christian Vision and the Modern Corporation*. Notre Dame: University of Notre Dame Press, 1982.

Yanagi, Soetsu. *The Unknown Craftsman: A Japanese Insight into Beauty*. New York: Kodansha, 1972.